AUDEL®

Complete Course in
STAINED GLASS

by Pepe Mendez

Macmillan Publishing Company

New York

Collier Macmillan Publishers

London

DEDICATION: I dedicate this book to all who love the beauty of stained glass.

The author, Pepe Mendez, has his studio in Tulsa, Oklahoma, and since he came to this country he has executed over 100 commissions. The major part of his work is in the theological field and most of his work has been with church windows. He has over 20 years' of experience and his work is not limited to stained glass. He has worked in mosaic byzantine tile, faceted glass, concrete sculpture, and all the derivatives of stained glass. Today he is considered one of the outstanding artists in the stained glass field. Being a painter and sculptor, he has found in stained glass the perfect medium in which he can express himself.

TABLE OF CONTENTS

LESSON 1

TOOLS:

Glass cutter — figure 1, 2 and 3

Lead opener — figure 4

Pliers (breaking pliers, grozing pliers) — figures 5 and 6

Lead vise — figure 7

Lead knife — figure 8

X-acto knife — figure 9

Stanley knife — figure 10

Soldering iron — figure 11

Sponge — figure 12

Brushes (acid brush, cementing brush) — figures 13and 14

Nails — figure 15

Hammer (light) — figure 16

Pattern cutter (pattern shears, double knife, double blades)—figures 17, 18 and 19

MATERIALS:

Glass (plate, antique, roll, opalescent, impresso)

Paper (for pattern)

Lead

Oleic acid

Solder (40-60)

Kerosene

Light oil

Caulking compound (DAP 1012)

Whiting

WHEEL
FIG. 1

WHEELS
FIG. 2

WHEELS
FIG. 3

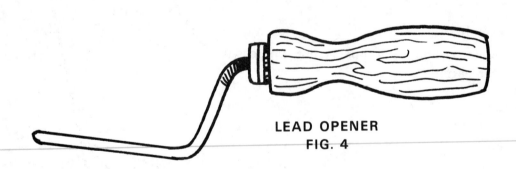

LEAD OPENER
FIG. 4

BRAKING PLIERS
FIG. 5

GROZING PLIERS
FIG. 6

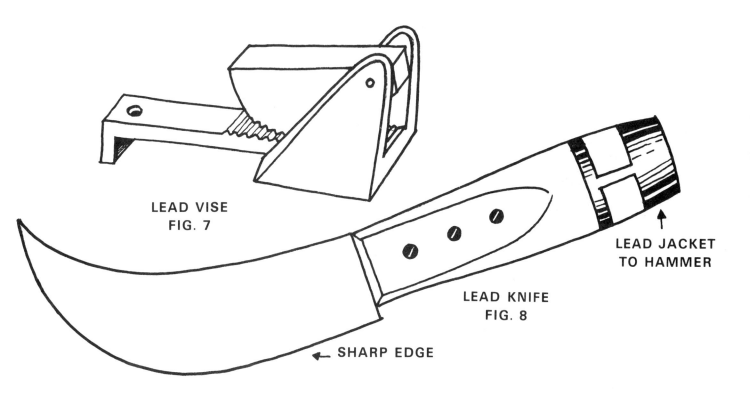

LEAD VISE
FIG. 7

LEAD JACKET
TO HAMMER

LEAD KNIFE
FIG. 8

← SHARP EDGE

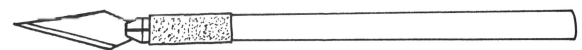

X-ACTO KNIFE
FIG. 9

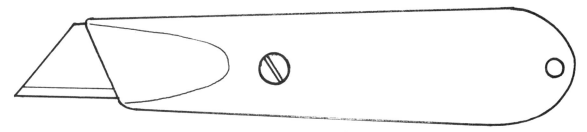

STANLEY KNIFE
FIG. 10

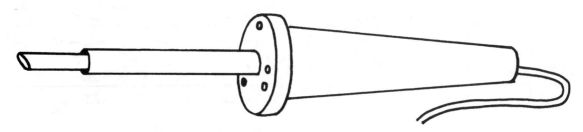

SOLDERING IRON 40 WTS.
FIG. 11

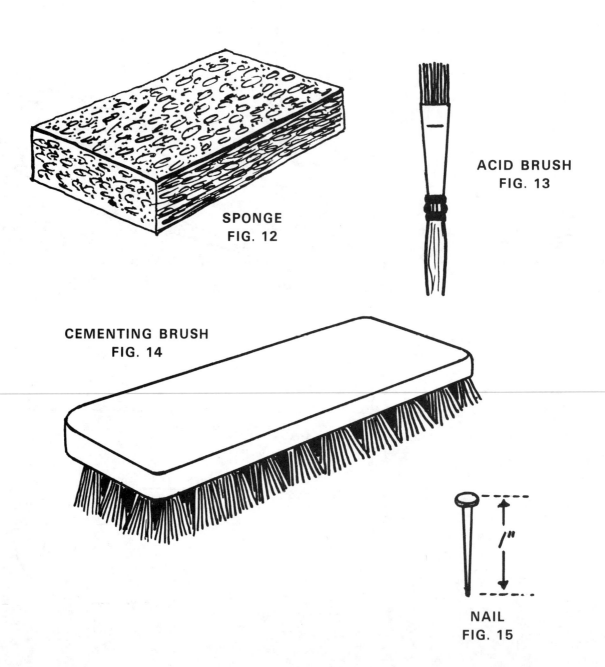

SPONGE
FIG. 12

ACID BRUSH
FIG. 13

CEMENTING BRUSH
FIG. 14

1"

NAIL
FIG. 15

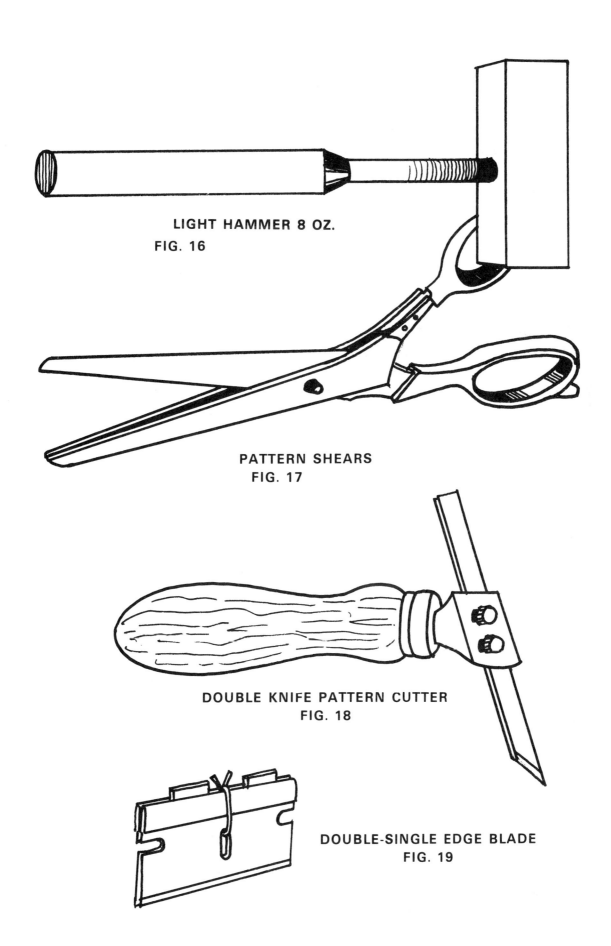

LIGHT HAMMER 8 OZ.
FIG. 16

PATTERN SHEARS
FIG. 17

DOUBLE KNIFE PATTERN CUTTER
FIG. 18

DOUBLE-SINGLE EDGE BLADE
FIG. 19

GLOSSARY

1. **Assemble:** To put together pieces of glass with lead
2. **Antique Glass:** Glass made by the hand-blown technique
3. **Beading:** Applying a bead of solder to copper foil pieces
4. **Blank Glass:** Piece of uncut glass from which a pattern is cut
5. **Came:** Strip of lead used to hold the glass pieces together
6. **Cartooning:** Working, painting or drawing of the project, usually full-sized
7. **Cementing:** Method of filling the grooves of lead to strengthen and waterproof the piece
8. **Flux:** Any chemical product for cleaning the joints in soldering, such as oleic acid
9. **Foiling:** Wrapping a strip of copper foil around a piece of glass
10. **Grozer:** Tool used in shaping and cutting glass
11. **Lathekin:** Tool made of wood used to open the groove of the lead came
12. **Lead Came:** Strip of lead milled to a specific shape and size
13. **Leading:** Putting pieces of glass together by the use of lead came
14. **Lead Joint:** Where pieces of lead butt together

15. **Patina Antique:** Treatment of solder with copper sulfate solution
16. **Pattern:** Piece of paper with a specific form that is used to cut a blank of glass
17. **Panel:** Completed section of glass and lead that is already assembled
18. **Roll Glass:** Opalescent glass
19. **Score:** Action of marking the glass blank with a glass cutter
20. **Section:** Definite part of a working project (panel, lamp, etc.)
21. **Solder:** Material used in the joining of two pieces — usually 40% tin, 60% lead; also, 50% tin and 50% lead
22. **Soldering Iron:** Tool which, through heat at its tip, melts solder and joins pieces of lead
23. **Stained Glass:** Glass composed of silicon sand, soda ash, limestone, borax, plus iron and other metalic oxides to obtain a definite color
24. **Tack Solder:** Technique of dropping a drop of solder when assembling, for the purpose of adjustment in the project that is being assembled
25. **Template:** A specific shape of a pattern cut out, from which a definite piece of glass will be cut
26. **Tinning:** A coat of solder on the tip of the iron to make it workable
27. **Whiting:** Calcium carbonate (powdered chalk) used to clean and dry panels after caulking or cementing

GLASS CUTTER:

There are several on the market, but I advise you to start with the single wheel cutter and to have several different numbers, such as #2, #4, and #6, for different glass types. When not in use, keep your cutting wheel clean and oiled by soaking in a mixture of kerosene and light oil. Baby food jars are very handy for this. There are other cutters such as shown in figures 2 and 3, that can be used as you become more experienced. Since they have multiple wheels they are more economical Never keep a cutter that is not sharp. When it is not making a good score, throw it away and use a new one. (It is more expensive to spoil a piece of glass than to throw away a cutter.) When it makes an interrupted line this will indicate it is time to throw your cutter away.

LEAD OPENER: FIG 4

You can use an old screwdriver. Cut or grind the tip to a point, bend it at an angle and it will be equal to the type sold for the craft. Also, you can sharpen a piece of hard wood and use it for a lead opener. Sometimes I can't find mine and I use the blunt end of my glass cutter and it works quite well. Always dampen the opener in kerosene before you insert it in the groove of the lead. This will make it run easily.

PLIERS: FIG 5 and 6

Flare grip jaw pliers #3410 from CRL: This type is used for breaking glass. To accomplish this, you set the grip close to the scoring line and pull down. This will give you a clean break.

Grozing pliers: This type is used to chew unwanted bits or sections of glass. This tool is really useful when you have to do difficult cuts.

LEAD VISE: FIG 7

When you are working alone, this is an indispensable tool. It can be ordered from the CRL catalogue #34. You will save many times the price paid when it is used properly because of the saving in lead (lead is expensive). Remember to always set it at the opposite end of the working table so that you can pull your lead and set it for opening without interference. If you cannot find a lead vise, use two pliers, one at each end of the lead, and then pull. For a long piece of lead, have someone hold one end while you stretch it.

LEAD KNIFE: FIG 8

This, to me, is the most useful tool in the craft. It serves as a lead cutter, hammer, nail puller, glass tapper, and in setting windows into their openings. This tool can be ordered in CRL catalogue #LK — 4682. To use it for cutting lead, you have to use a rock-back-and-forth motion and exert a little pressure. This will always make a clean cut. It is wise to have a sharpening stone and occasionally sharpen the edge of the knife. It will then always be in top cutting shape. You can use an X-acto knife or a Stanley Blade Knife in place of a lead knife; however, these tools may be hard on your hands. FIG 9 and 10

SOLDERING IRON: FIG 11

This tool can be found almost anywhere — hardware stores, department stores, electrical supply stores, etc. It comes in a variety of wattages (40, 60, 80, 100, 120, 150, 200, etc.). Until you learn how to work with them it is advisable to use a low wattage iron. You will thus run less risk of burning a hole in the lead you are soldering. When using the soldering iron, always keep a wet celulose sponge close at hand. Once in a while run the tip into the sponge; this will clean the tip and extend its use. Another thing you should watch is the temperature at the tip of the iron. If you heat it for as long as eight to ten minutes before you use it to solder, try it out on a scrap of lead. By doing this, you will find if it is too hot for use. If so, it will melt the scrap and, by observing this, you can prevent the burning of a hole in the piece you are soldering. If it is too hot, cool it by dipping it into the sponge and then solder.

SPONGE: FIG 12

Any celulose sponge such as those available in super markets or discounts stores will do the job. Place it in a plate full of water near the area in which you will be soldering. It will then be handy at all times to clean the tip or to cool the iron.

BRUSHES: FIG 15

Any cheap brush will do for applying oleic acid. The cementing brush should not be very hard, nor should it be extremely soft (shoe polishing brushes are great for this).

NAILS: FIG

All work in stained-leaded glass is put together with nails. Do not use nails that are too small or too large; 1" or 1 1/4" with heads are good for this use. Remember to use a lot of nails when assembling any piece. The better the pieces of glass are secured, the better the final product will be.

HAMMER: FIG. 16

A good 4 or 6 ounce light hammer with a flat head will be a useful tool in assembling. Do not use a round head hammer or a bigger hammer because if it slips when striking a nail it will hit and break the glass. If this happens in the beginning or at the end it is a minor problem to solve; simply cut and set a new piece of glass. But if it happens in the middle of the assembly, it will involve a lot of time and work to replace the piece that was hit.

PATTERN CUTTERS: FIG. 17

This tool is very useful in the stained glass craft. The most common is the pattern shears. This will give you the same cutout allowance for the heart of the lead came every time. Other substitutions such as illustrated in figures 18 and 19 will vary a little, depending on the pressure you exert. When assembling a window or a panel or any other piece, except Tiffany lamps, you will have to cut out sufficient allowance in the pattern to equal the heart of the lead. You will then have a perfect set of templates with which to work.

SUPPLIERS' ADDRESSES:
TOOLS:

CR Laurence Company, Inc., 1425 Tonne Road, Elk Grove Village, Illinois 60007, telephone number: (312) 437-8320.

GLASS ANTIQUE:

Blenko Glass Company, Milton, West Virginia 25541, telephone number: (304) 743-9081.

S. A. Bendheim Company, Inc., 122 Hudson Street, Corner North Moore Street, New York, New York 10013, telephone number: (212) 226-6370 and 226-6371.

GLASS DOMESTIC:

Kokomo Opalescent Glass Company, Inc., P.O. Box 809, Kokomo, Indiana 46901, telephone number: (317) 457-8136.

Paul Wissmach Glass Company, Inc., Paden City, West Virginia 26159, telephone number: (304) 337-2253.

LEAD:

Crown Metal Company, 117 E. Washington Street, Milwaukee, Wisconsin 53205, telephone number: (414) 384-6500.

Gardiner Metal Company, 4820 So. Campbell Avenue, Chicago, Illinois 60632, telephone number: (312) 847-0100.

ACID:

Any chemical company in your locality.

COMPOUND CEMENTING 1012:

Any glass company in your locality.

SOLDER:

Any plumbing distribution company in your locality.

THINNER:

Any paint shop or hardware store in your locality.

WHITING:

Any paint shop or hardware store in your locality.

SUPPLIES, MATERIALS AND TOOLS ALSO AVAILABLE, FOR PURCHASE AT MY STUDIO AT:
2714 E. 15th St.
TULSA, OKLAHOMA 74104
Phone 918—939-2969

LESSON 2
HOW TO HOLD GLASS CUTTERS,
HOW TO CUT GLASS

In any trade or craft, the first thing to do is to learn the proper handling of the tools you will use. In stained glass, the most important tool is the glass cutter. There are several cutters available. I have found that Fletcher's cutters have been best for me. It is important to learn the different types of glass and their properties before you undertake cutting glass.

The easiest glass to cut is common plate glass of single strength. Next easiest is antique or mouthblown glass. This type of glass is only manufactured by one company in this country, Blenko Glass Company, Milton, West Virginia 25541, telephone number (304) 743-9081. It is more expensive than the other, but it has about the same easy scoring quality as plate glass. There is also European antique glass, which is produced in Europe, and is distributed here by Bienefeld Industries, Inc., 1539 Covert Street, Brooklyn, New York 11227, telephone number (212) 821-4400, and S. A. Bendheim Company, Inc., 122 Hudson Street, Corner North Moore Street, New York, New York 10013, telephone number (212) 226-6370 and 226-6371. This is a high-quality and expensive glass. Third is the domestic rolled glass with similar properties of antique glass, although it is manufactured in a different way. This type of glass is produced by Kokomo Opalescent Glass Company, Inc., P. O. Box 809, Kokomo, Indiana 46901, telephone number (317) 457-8136, and Paul Wissmach Glass Company, Inc., Paden City, West Virginia 26159, telephone number (304) 337-2253. These companies manufacture other types of glass, such as impresso, roundel and glass more commonly known in the lamp manufacturing business as opalescent. This particular type of glass is the hardest glass to cut.

It is advisable to find samples of the different types of glass and try to cut them in order to learn the properties of each type. Also, some glass has one smooth face and one textured face. Always cut the glass on the smooth face. The only type with which this general rule does not apply is flash glass, which has a layer of color in one of its faces. It is hard to cut on the face with the color pigment. This glass will cut easily on the back side.

Once you have selected your glass, the next step is to start scoring and breaking. For round cuts or curves, it is better to use a smaller wheel, such as a #2; for straight cuts, a bigger wheel, like #4; and for hard glass, a #6 cutter. Glass cutters can be purchased in any glass company in your locality. There are other cutters, like diamond or carborundum, but they are expensive and the wheel cutter will do the same job and cost less. Find a good size piece of plate glass (10'' x 20''), and set it on a level table. If possible, find a piece of smoothly woven rug on which to set the glass. Some rug companies will sell their old samples. If a rug is not available, use several newspapers and set the glass on top of them. This will give you a cushion on which you can press down. Now you are ready to try to score.

Take the glass cutter, as shown in figure A, between the index and middle fingers, resting the thumb on the back side of the cutter. Hold the cutter almost vertical to the glass. If you score properly you will hear a hissing sound. Now the glass is ready to break. Place your index fingers of both hands under the glass on both sides of and parallel to the scoring line. Figure B The closer you can get to the scoring line of the glass, the better. Keeping a firm grip and exerting a little pressure, snap or pull down on the glass and the glass will break apart in a clean line. Figure C. Repeat the same motion of scoring and breaking several times. Always be sure that your scoring line goes from end to end or border to border as shown in figure D, not as figure E. If the line is not the same along the full length it will not give a perfect break and you will run the risk of breaking the glass in any direction. After several cuts in this manner, try holding the cutter as in Figure F. Place the cutter between the index finger and thumb, resting the index finger in the depression of the cutter as shown in figures J and K. Repeat, making several scores and breaking. By now you will know which position is best for you and with which of the two ways of holding the cutter you feel more at ease. I personally use both; as shown in figure A, when I am scoring from top to bottom; and as in figure F, when scoring from bottom to top.

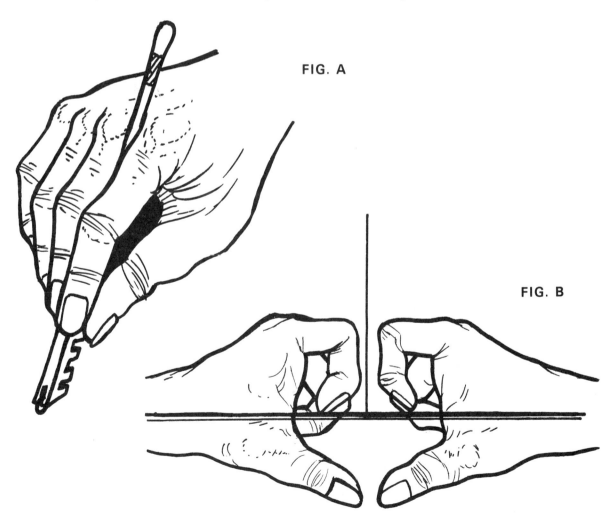

FIG. A

FIG. B

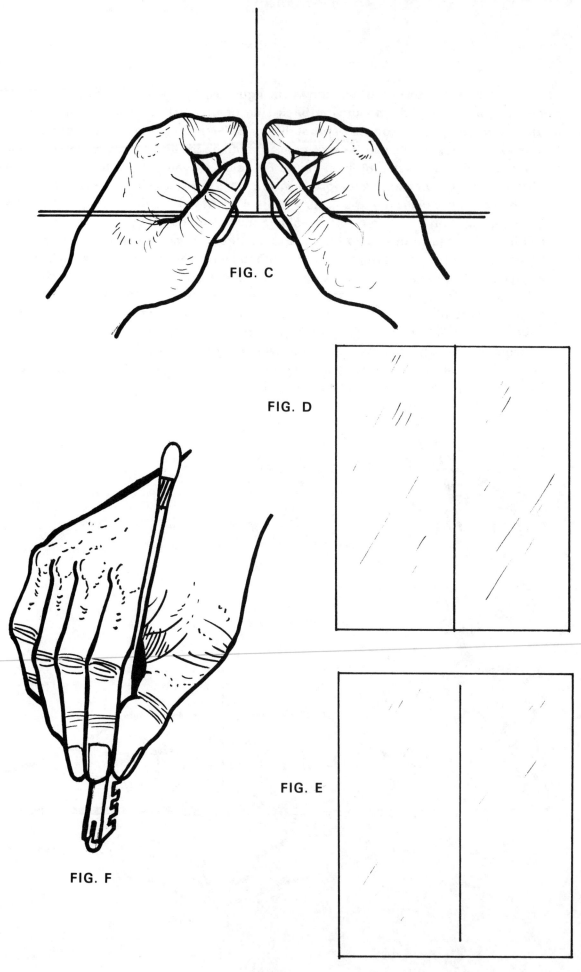

FIG. C

FIG. D

FIG. E

FIG. F

Now, try curved lines. Begin with small curves and after awhile progress to deeper curves. If a good score is made, curves will break in the same manner as straight lines. The next thing to learn is to tap the glass. This done when you are cutting glass that is hard or a curve that will be difficult to snap. First, score a line; then take your glass cutter as in figure I and, with the other hand, take the glass and hold it. Start tapping the score line from underneath. Do not hit it too hard because you may break the glass into pieces. Also, do not tap so softly that it will not make the break or a running line. Practice and you will see that the glass will separate or break easily.

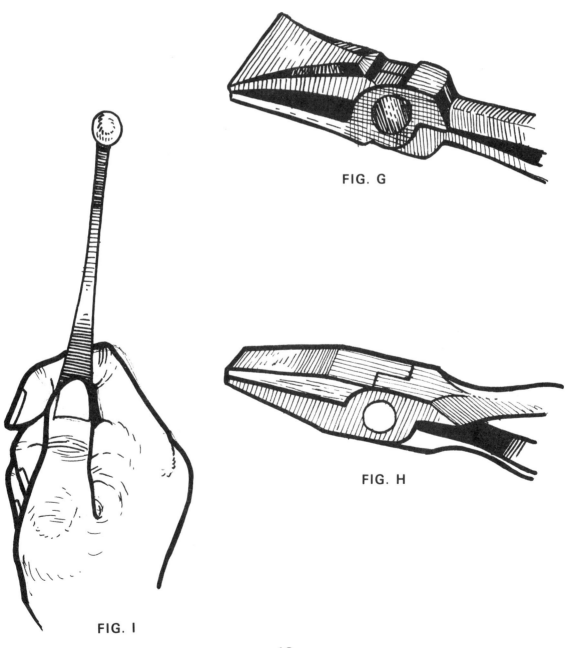

FIG. G

FIG. H

FIG. I

Sometimes you will have to use a glass-pliers. There are the breaking pliers, the one with the wide or flaired mouth, and the grozing pliers, the one with the flat jaws and smaller head. These tools are really useful in working with glass and you should be able to buy them from C. R. Laurence Company, Inc., 1425 Tonne Road, Elk Grove Village, Illinois 60007, telephone number: (312) 437-8320. These glass pliers are shown in figures G. and H. The breaking pliers are for breaking some difficult scores that neither snapping with fingers nor tapping will accomplish. Hold them parallel to the score line and snap. The grozing pliers are for shaping glass in some cuts that are really difficult to do otherwise. (see figure L) You will notice that score lines have been made for cutting away segments A, B and C of the glass. However segment D must be removed by using the grozing pliers after the score line has been made. Exert sufficient pressure to crush small portions of glass between the score line of the last break of segment C and the final score line of segment D in the grozing area. Remember that the reason for using this grozing technique is the difficulty of the cut and do not attempt to break off any large pieces with the grozing pliers in the grozing area. To do so would result in a breaking of the glass beyond the desired line.

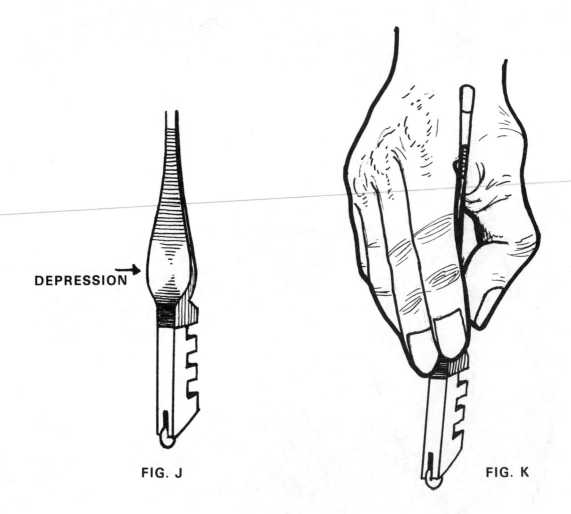

DEPRESSION

FIG. J

FIG. K

Sometimes you will need to cut a circle or similar type of pattern. The way to do this is shown in figure M. Line 1 should be scored as a continuation of the arc of the circle and broken. Line 2 should then be scored as a continuation of the arc of the circle to the top edge of the blank and to the point where the segment of glass was broken off after the scoring of the line 1, and broken. Line 3 should then be scored as a continuation of the arc of the circle to the left edge of the blank and to the point where the segment of glass was broken off after the scoring of line 2, and broken. This should be repeated with lines 4 and 5. By using this method you minimize the possibility of breakage. I would like to point out at this stage that you should always use a blank, from which you will cut the pattern you want. Always allow a little more room on your blank than the pattern calls for (see figures N, O and P). If you have followed all these procedures correctly in cutting glass, you are now ready to start your first project. You are now on your way to the pleasure of the stained glass craft.

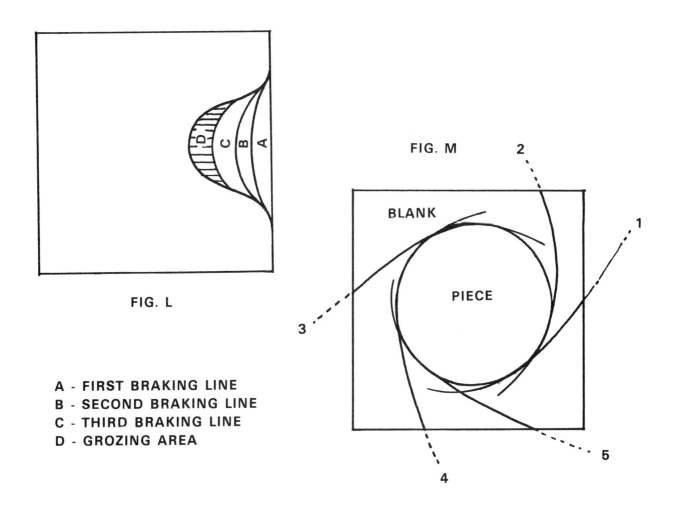

FIG. L

FIG. M

BLANK

PIECE

2

1

3

4

5

A - FIRST BRAKING LINE
B - SECOND BRAKING LINE
C - THIRD BRAKING LINE
D - GROZING AREA

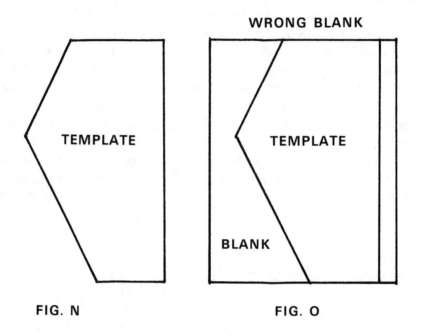

FIG. N

WRONG BLANK

FIG. O

RIGTH SIZE OF BLANK

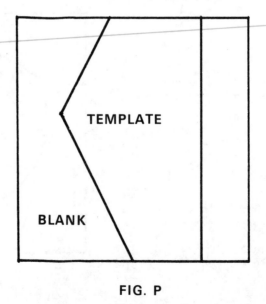

FIG. P

LESSON 3
CARTOON AND PATTERN
DRAWING THE PATTERN — STUDY OF LEAD CAME

When we discuss cartooning, we mean the drawing of any design or idea to the actual size we want to produce. This is a very careful drawing and is done with charcoal or pencil. When done to our satisfaction, we will go over it with a felt tip ink pen to clearly define the drawing. Now we have established the size and shape of the piece we want to produce. In every pattern there are always three lines to take into consideration. The first line is the outside line; the second, the glass line; and the third, the showing of the glass line (see figure Q). Always be careful to take these three lines into consideration when doing a pattern or cartoon. If you do not, you will end up with an oversized piece when you have finished assembling. You will always need two copies of your cartoon, one for assembling and the other for cutting out the templates. To accomplish this, take two pieces of heavy bond paper interleaved with two pieces of carbon paper, and place them under the cartoon. Secure them to your work table with masking tape (see figure R), and start going over the lines carefully. Be sure you have all the lines drawn. After you have finished drawing all the lines, go over and number each piece and indicate the color on each piece so you will know where it goes and also what color it is to be when you cut the glass with the templates. The way to number and put the colors on the pattern is explained in the next lesson (figure 22). Now you are ready to cut your pattern pieces.

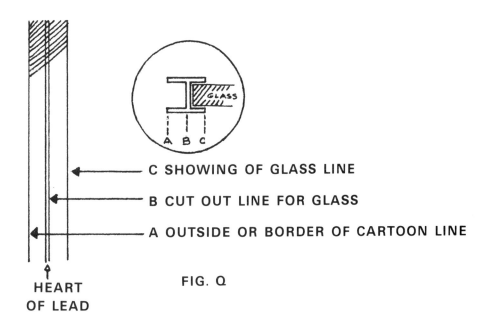

C SHOWING OF GLASS LINE

B CUT OUT LINE FOR GLASS

A OUTSIDE OR BORDER OF CARTOON LINE

HEART
OF LEAD

FIG. Q

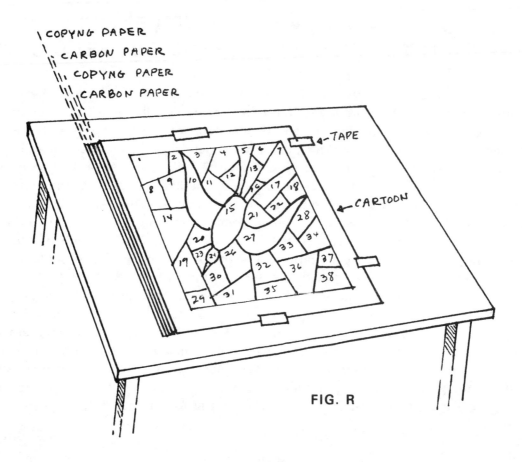

COPYNG PAPER
CARBON PAPER
COPYNG PAPER
CARBON PAPER

←TAPE

←CARTOON

FIG. R

First, select one of the copies and set it aside. That will be your assembling pattern and the other will be the one you will use to cut out and make templates for cutting the pieces of glass. Next, trim the outside of the pattern to the glass edge line (see figures Q and R). Then with a pattern shears or with two single-edged blades, as illustrated in figures 17 and 19, cut the center of every line. By doing this you are allowing for the heart of the lead (see figure Q). When you finish cutting all your templates they must be checked against the assembling pattern to see if they fit correctly. This is the advantage of pattern shears because you get a cut-out line every time. Then group the templates by colors, that is, all the reds together, etc. Use an old magazine and put every color group of templates together between the pages. This reduces the chance of loosing or misplacing them. Now you are ready to start cutting your glass.

LEAD CAME: In the old days, people used to mill their own lead cames and some studios still do this today; however, this process is tedious and long. It is easier to buy the lead in strips from any studio or glass company in your locality. If not available at a studio, you can order the lead came from a manufacturer — I use Crown Metal Company, 121 Washington Street, Milwaukee, Wisconsin 53204, telephone number (414) 384-6500.

Determine the size of lead you will use. For small pieces you need small lead and for bigger pieces you probably will have to mix your sizes. Types of lead came available vary from 3/16 U channel to 1 1/2 H channels. There are flat head, round

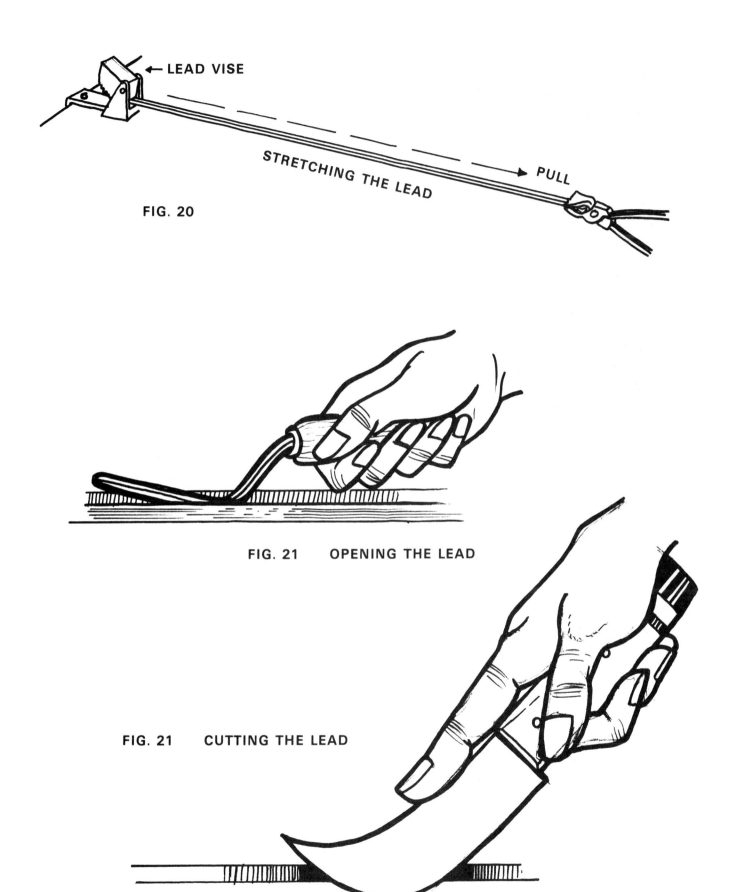

← LEAD VISE

STRETCHING THE LEAD ▸ PULL

FIG. 20

FIG. 21   OPENING THE LEAD

FIG. 21   CUTTING THE LEAD

head and reinforced heads. Lead is sold by weight and by boxes of 100 pounds and 130 pounds, and cost approximately 50 cents to 65 cents per pound. You should always stretch your lead after removing it from the box. To do this, use your lead vise (figure 7). Nail the vise to the edge of the work table; insert your lead; press the head down; and, using your glass pliers, pull the strip of lead from the other end (figure 20). By doing this, your lead will stretch and straighten out. Now you have to open it with a lead opener (figure 4), a lathekin, the back of your cutter, or a piece of wood. Run the opener between the lips of the came and inside the groove the full length of the strip (figure 21). Do this to both sides so it wll be easy to insert the pieces of glass when you start assembling. When you begin assembling, it is advisable to cut the full length of the lead came into two or three short lengths so it wil be easier to handle. The most commonly used lead is 3/8'' round head came. This type of lead is used in windows and is also the most commonly used in the manufacturing of lamps, terrariums, candle boxes, etc. I would suggest at this point that you proceed slowly in your learning process. Do not try to assimilate everything in one day or week. If you pace yourself to one lesson per week you will do fine and by the end of the first month you will be producing good work. If you rush your learning process you will not learn properly and will spoil a lot of glass and material. You should go over each lesson at least twice and plan everything with the slow-but-sure pace that it takes to learn the stained glass art.

LESSON 4
CUTTING PATTERN AND
GLASS-ASSEMBLING, CEMENTING

Take two pieces of carbon paper and two pieces of heavy brown paper, a file folder or any other type of heavy paper, and place it under the pattern (pattern #1). Trace it with a pencil, going over the lines very carefully. When the tracing is finished, number the pattern from left to right and top to bottom, and write on the pattern the colors you have selected for each piece (figure 22). Now you are ready to cut your pattern.

Take one of the two copies and trim the outside with a scissors or a blade. Then cut your patterns with the pattern shears. For this particular design you will need only templates #1, 2, 4, 6, 7, 13 and 14, because the rest of the templates are repeated in the design. Be sure you cut the patterns in the center of the lines to allow for the thickness of the heart of the lead to be cut out. After you have done this, check the patterns cut out with the assembling pattern and check for proper fit. Group the patterns by color and write on them the number of pieces needed. (Example: Of piece #1 there are only two, but of piece #6 there are four, two in each color and also rights and lefts.) Constantly check and recheck the pattern against the master assembling pattern to avoid any mistake.

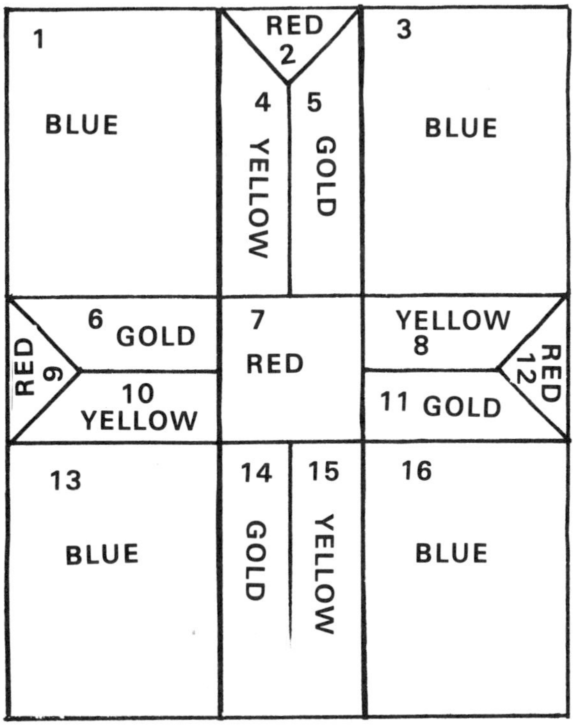

FIG. 22

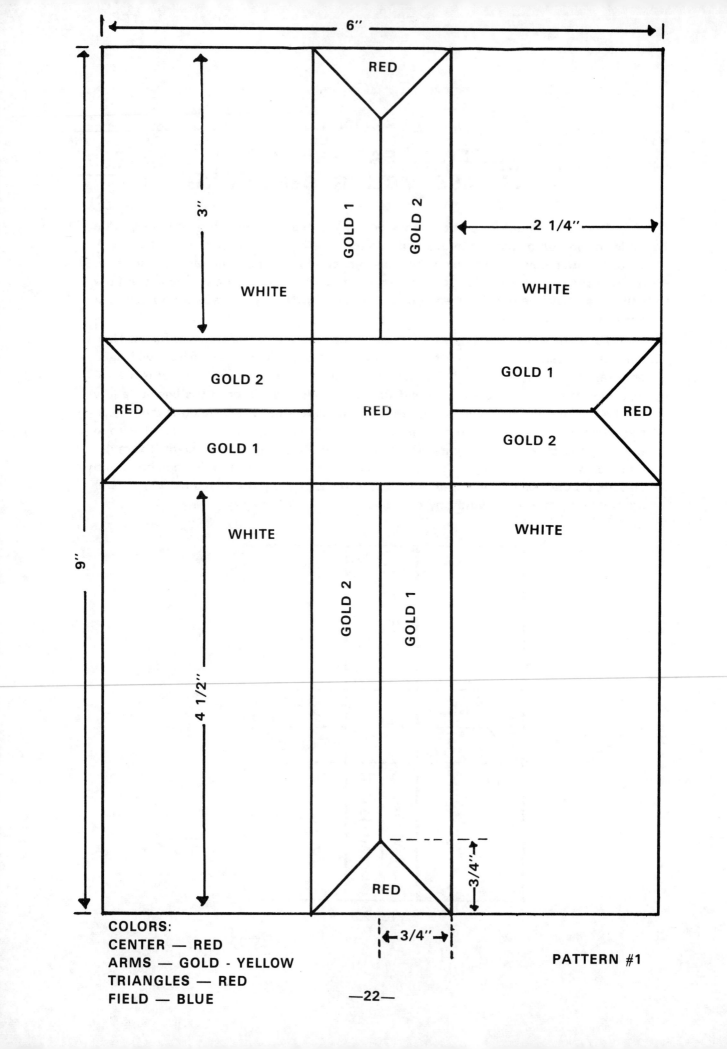

6"

RED

GOLD 1   GOLD 2

3"

WHITE   2 1/4"   WHITE

GOLD 2   GOLD 1

RED   RED   RED

GOLD 1   GOLD 2

9"

WHITE   WHITE

GOLD 2   GOLD 1

4 1/2"

3/4"

RED

3/4"

COLORS:
CENTER — RED
ARMS — GOLD - YELLOW
TRIANGLES — RED
FIELD — BLUE

PATTERN #1

—22—

Now you are ready to start cutting glass. Select the first color you want to cut and cut out as many blanks as you need. Then place the paper pattern on top of the blank and score the glass, being careful to follow the contour of the pattern, or template. After scoring the piece, break it and you will have your first piece. Check it with the master pattern and do the same with the remaining pieces. Check each piece to see if it fits as closely as possible. If not, you will have to adjust it. When you have cut all the pieces to your satisfaction you are ready to assemble.

The first thing you will have to do is find a place to lay your master assembling pattern (the copy that you did not cut). A wooden table or a large piece of plywood would make a good place for assembling. Then take two pieces of wood (1" x 3/4" x 12" and 1" x 3/4" x 8" and, using nails with heads (1" or 1 1/4"), nail the pieces of wood at a right angle at th edge of the cut-out line (see figure 23).

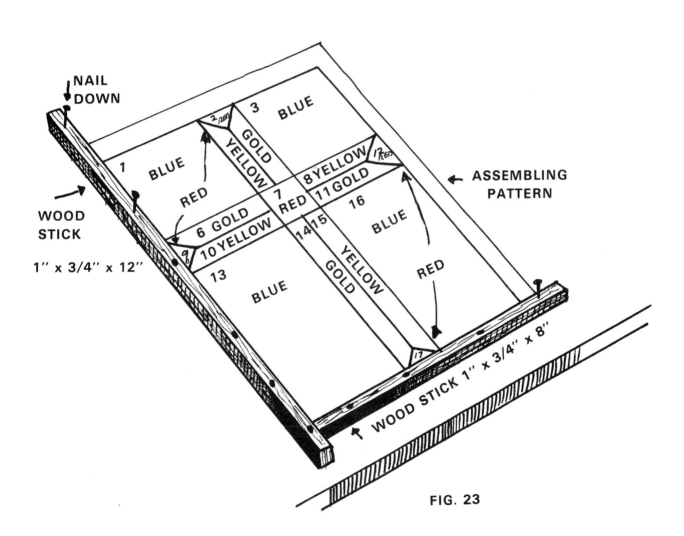

FIG. 23

—23—

When the boards are firm in place, take the piece of H Channel lead you are going to use (3/8") and stretch it in the lead vise. If you do not have a lead vise, use two pliers, one on each end, and pull. Then open the lead with a lathekin or lead opener (the back of your cutter will do) on both sides. Cut two lengths of lead slightly over the full length of the pattern's sides and nail the ends to the table or plywood, forming a corner (see figure 24). You are ready to put your first piece of glass, #13, in your assembling pattern. Set the piece of glass inside the groove of the two leads in angle, and be sure it is in all the way. Nail at the top with three nails against the edge of the glass, holding the piece in place (figure 25). Set in a piece of H-Channel lead, 1/8" shorter than the length of the glass, and set it in the edge of the glass that is not nailed, putting a couple of nails there to hold it in place (figure 26).

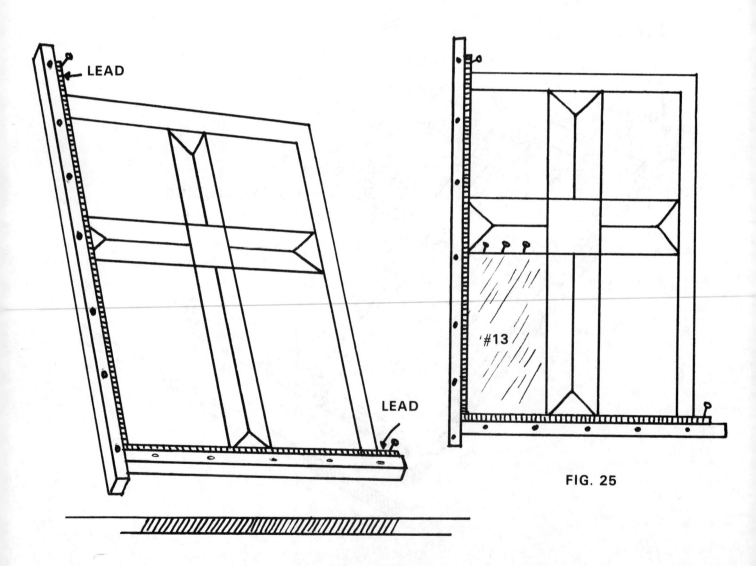

LEAD

LEAD

#13

FIG. 25

FIG. 24

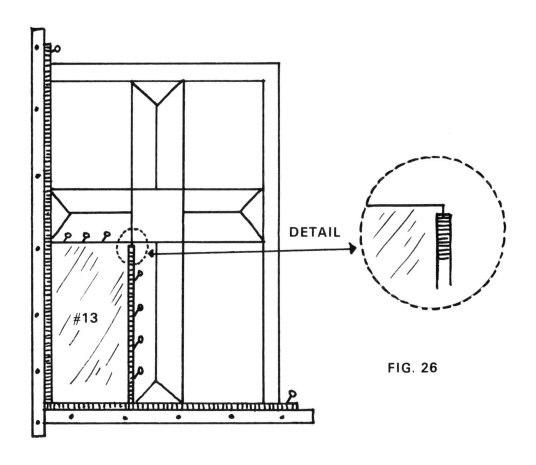

DETAIL

#13

FIG. 26

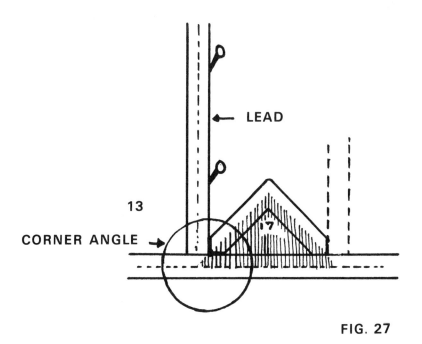

LEAD

13

CORNER ANGLE ➤

FIG. 27

—25—

Now you are ready for your second piece, #17. This piece being in an angle, you will have to cut the lead at an angle equal to the corner and also 1/8" shorter than the length of the glass (figure 27). To accomplish this, bend a piece of lead around the piece of glass (figure 28), you are going to set in and with your lead knife or other tool you are using, make a cut at the angle shown. Always remember to allow 1/8" of glass showing at each end of the piece of glass and set it in place, pushing it all the way in. After you have cut the lead to the proper size, set the piece of glass with the lead around it in place, and nail it at the side on which you are not going to work. Then pull out the nails at the edge against which you are going to set your next piece of glass, (#14) and set the piece in (figure 29).

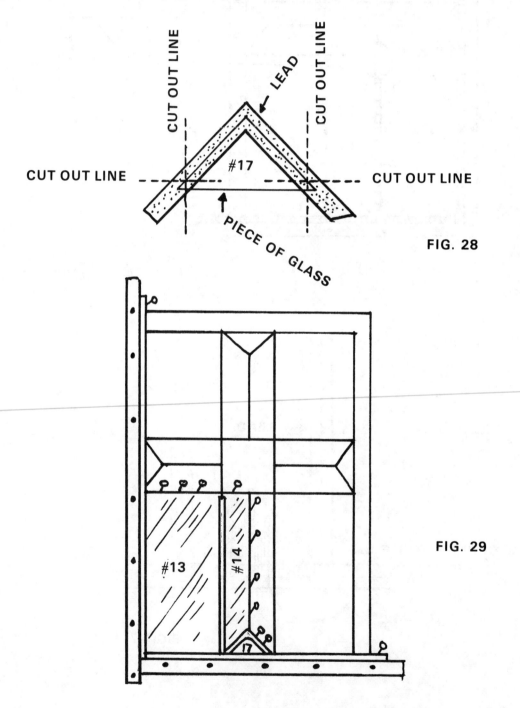

FIG. 28

FIG. 29

Cut a piece of lead to fit the length of the piece (#14), but always remember to allow 1/8" of the glass showing on top. Set the lead in place and nail the glass from the top, then pull out the nails at the edge of the base of the triangle and set in piece #15. Repeat the cutting and setting of the lead as previously indicated (figure 29). Then set piece #16, always nailing the pieces you are setting at the top (figure 30). When piece #16 is in place, nail at the right edge and pull all the other nails out (figure 31). Now you are ready to lead the full width of the pattern, always allowing 1/8" to show at the end of the glass (figure 31). Set piece #9, repeating the procedure used in setting #17, and then #10 and #6 in the same manner as #14 and #15, remembering to nail at the edge that you are not leading. Follow the same technique until you have all the pieces set in place and nailed at the border edges.

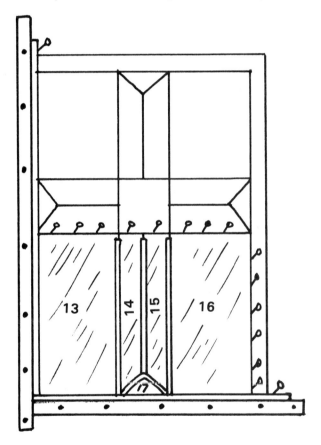

FIG. 30

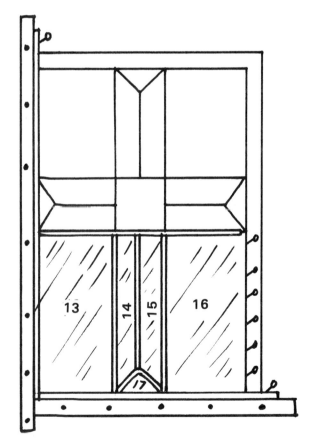

FIG. 31

Now you are ready to close the piece. Cut a length of lead for the top, following the same technique of allowing 1/8" showing on the glass. Complete the vertical length by placing the closing lead in place, which should be a little longer than the full dimension (figure 32), and nail it in place. Now you can use another piece of wood and gently set it against the outer edge of the lead (a wooden yard stick will do) and hit it in the side with the light hammer or the back of the lead knife. To straighten all the lines, do this on top and sides, then nail along the edge and you will be ready to solder.

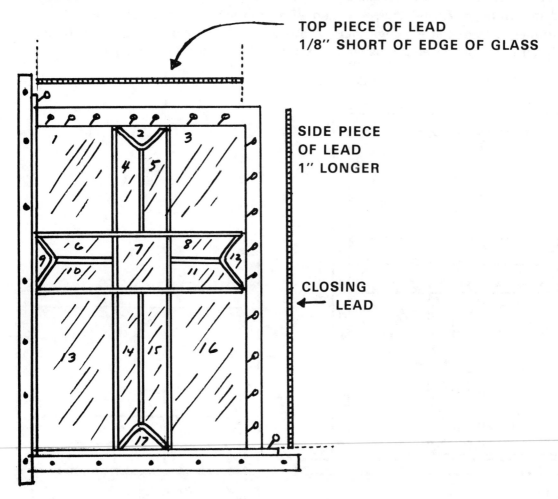

TOP PIECE OF LEAD
1/8" SHORT OF EDGE OF GLASS

SIDE PIECE
OF LEAD
1" LONGER

CLOSING
LEAD

FIG. 32

SOLDERING: You should use a 60-40 type of solder (40% tin-60% lead) and oleic acid at every point to be soldered. Have available a celulose sponge well soaked with water. Set the sponge at one side of the work table and plug in your iron. Use a 40 wts., 60 wts., or 80 wts. iron. When the iron is hot, put a small amount of solder on its tip to tin the tip. Clean the tip with the sponge and repeat the motion as many times as needed until the tip of the soldering iron is tinned completely (it will look bright and silvery). Hold the solder roll with one hand, allowing the end to extend approximately 4" and touching on top of the joint you want to solder. Then apply the tip of the iron on top of the end of the solder. Press a little and count to four, giving enough time for the heat to melt the solder and flow in the acid (figure 33).

Repeat this technique with all the joints you want to solder. Then, using a rag, wipe off the acid. Take all the nails out, turn the piece over and repeat the same steps on the other face. When you have finished, cut the excess of the closing end of the lead and you are ready to cement and antique the piece.

CEMENTING AND ANTIQUING: The first step is to mix the DAP 1012 compound with a little paint thinner. This glazing compound comes in a thick paste form and needs to be thinned. Use an empty can (coffee cans are very handy for this) and stir with a stick until the compound becomes runny. Then apply it with a cheap brush all over the piece. Now, using a medium hard brush (a shoe brush), brush the cement in all directions. Clean any excess in the brush you are using by wiping it on the edge of your table and continue brushing until you have it almost completely clean. Turn the piece over and repeat the process on the other side. When you have completed this, sprinkle a little whiting and brush the piece again. Go over the piece until it is completely clean and shiny. Repeat whiting procedure on the other face and your first piece will be completed. If you have any glass left, I recommend making the second pattern shown in this book (Pattern 2), using the same technique as in the first pattern.

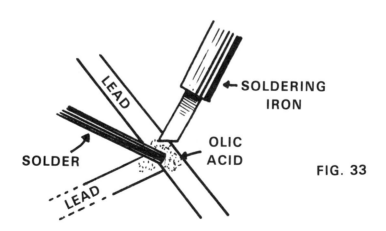

FIG. 33

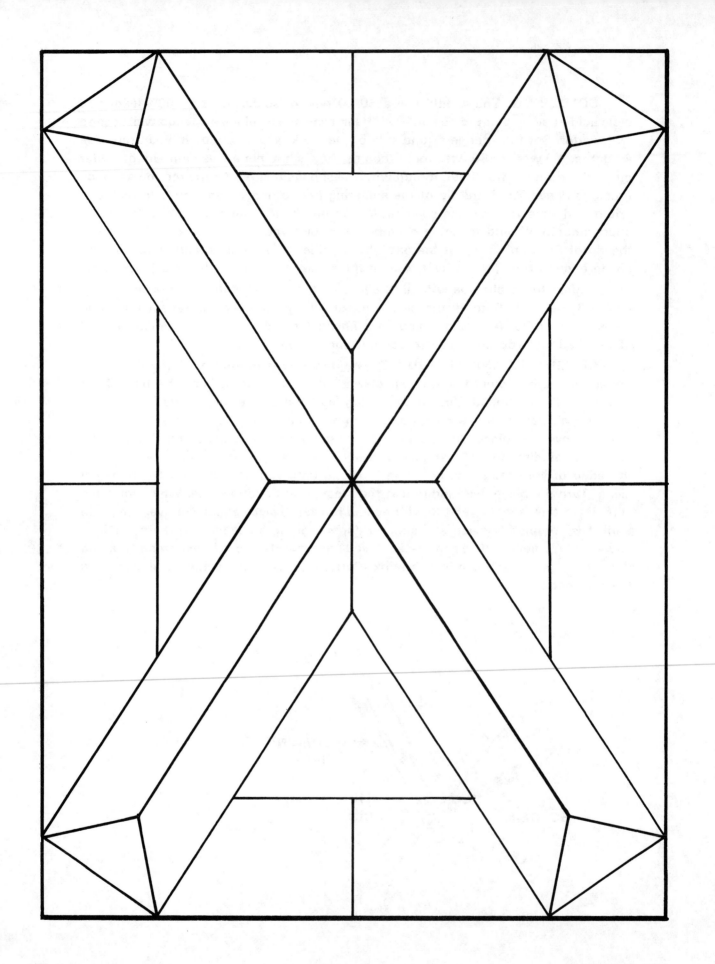

PATTERN #2

LESSON 5
SIMPLE MODEL LAMP, TWELVE SIDES INSTRUCTIONS

Using the same techniques as outlined in Lessons 3 and 4 for cartooning (drawing the pattern, cutting the pattern and cutting the glass pieces), you will be ready to make your first lamp. This will be a twelve-sided lamp, as shown in Pattern 3, with four variations of design to suit your own taste.

STEP 1. After you have cut your twelve pieces of glass, set them in the shape of a fan in front of you on your work table approximately 4" from the edge of the table. Nail the first piece (#1) on your left (figure 34) all the way around, top, side and bottom. Now take piece #2 and a piece of lead and measure the length you need. Always leave 3/32" on each end of the glass showing (see figure 35). Then cut eleven more pieces of the same length. Be sure your lead has been stretched and opened on both sides before you begin. Set the lead in the open side of piece #1 and set in piece #2. Tap lightly and nail it at both ends, making sure that the piece of glass does not move when you are nailing it. The best way to accomplish this is by nailing the open side with one nail and then nailing the bottom nails and the top nail. Then remove the side nail and shut in the second piece of lead. Repeat this procedure until you have all twelve pieces of glass in place. Put your last piece of lead at the end and secure it with nails (figure 36).

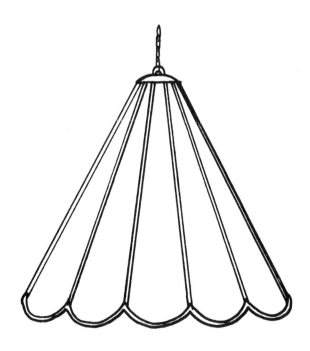

PATTERN #3

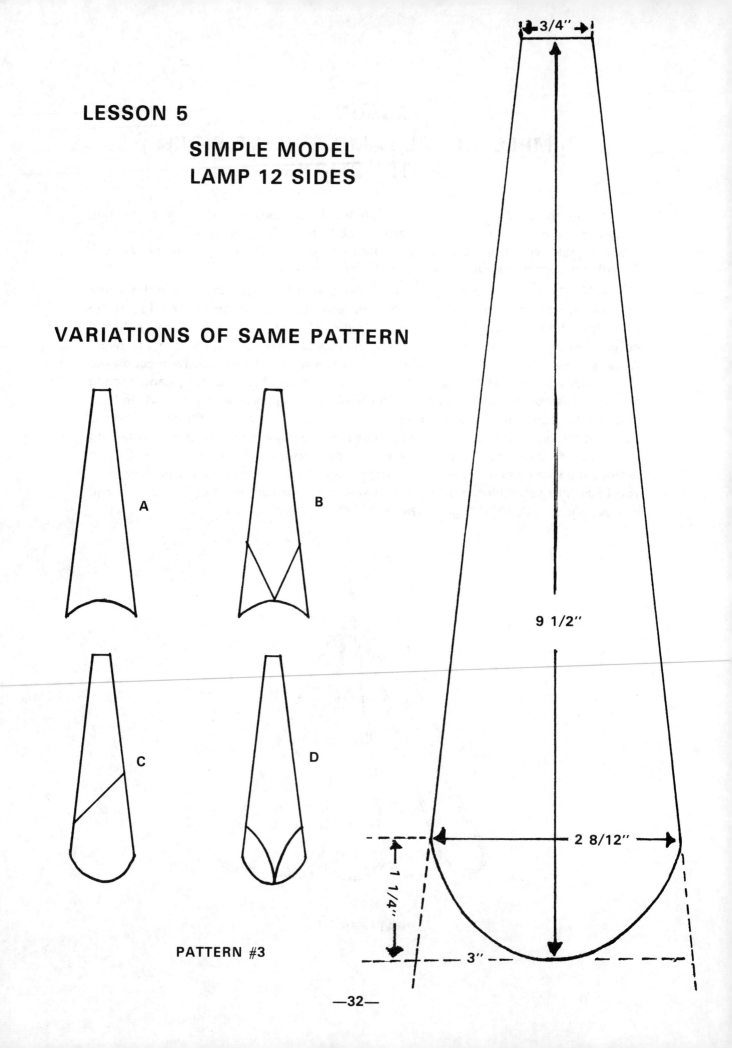

LESSON 5

**SIMPLE MODEL
LAMP 12 SIDES**

VARIATIONS OF SAME PATTERN

A

B

C

D

3/4"

9 1/2"

2 8/12"

1 1/4"

3"

PATTERN #3

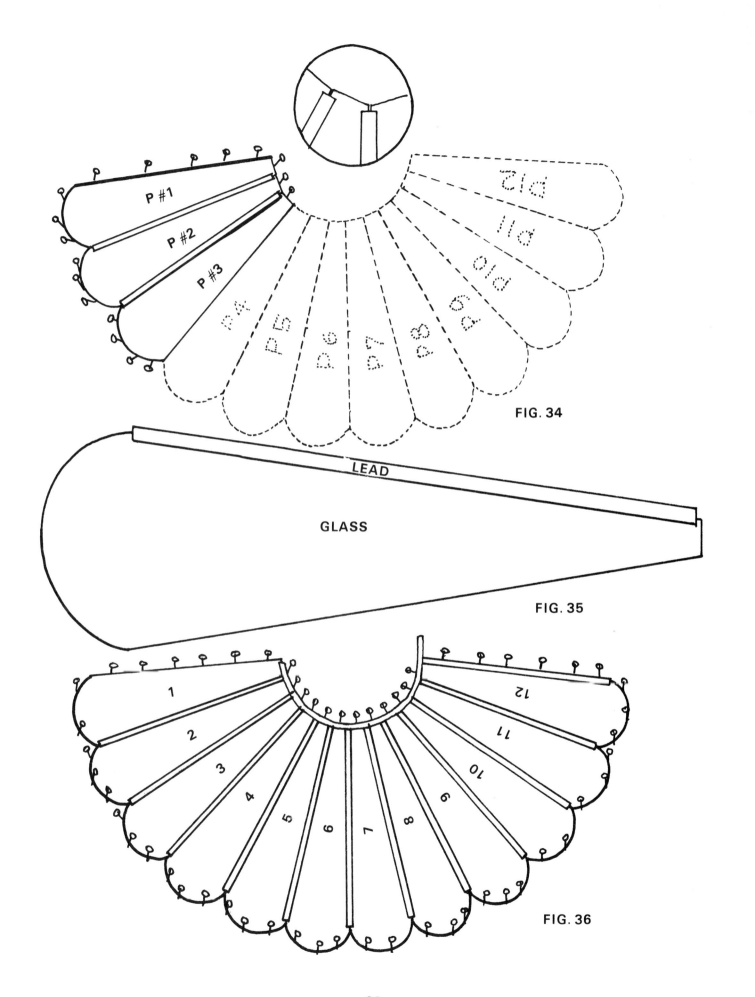

P #1

P #2

P #3

P #4

P #5

P #6

P #7

P #8

P #9

P #10

P #11

P #12

FIG. 34

LEAD

GLASS

FIG. 35

1

2

3

4

5

6

7

8

9

10

11

12

FIG. 36

STEP 2. Measure the top semi-circle and find how much lead you need. After doing this, cut a length of lead at least 2" longer than your measurement. Remove the nails from the top. Starting at the left top corner, push the lead, allowing 3/32" of glass to show. Put the lead in place around the semi-circle, pressing in every joint and secure with nails. Be sure your nails are well driven because you are now securing the top. You will be pushing from the bottom in your next step and the nails should provide a good support (figure 36).

STEP 3. Repeat the same procedure at the bottom. Do not remove all the nails at once. Just remove the nails from two pieces of glass (#1 and #2). After you have measured and cut the length of lead you need, place the lead from the left bottom corner, allowing 3/32" of glass to show. Nail against the lead and repeat the same procedure until you have secured the bottom semi-circle (figure 37). Press in the lead at the joints around the curve either with a piece of wood that fits in the groove of the lead or your lead opener. You are now ready for soldering.

STEP 4. Flux all the joints with oleic acid, using the brush, and solder the same way you soldered in previous lessons. Do not forget to count to four every time you touch the tip over the solder at the joint. After you have finished one side, turn the piece over and solder the other side in the same manner. The only precaution is not to run solder into the open end of the top and bottom pieces of lead. Now you are ready to put together the two ends.

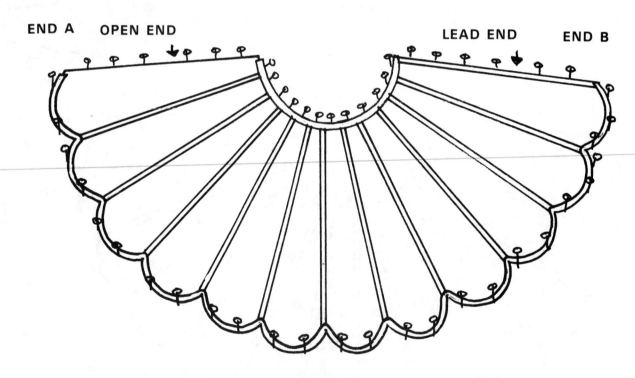

END A   OPEN END   LEAD END   END B

FIG. 37

STEP 5. Stand the piece on the bottom edge and start bending little by little, always being careful to bend at the joint of the two pieces of glass (figure 38). Bend until the two sides meet. If the lamp has been constructed according to the above instructions, end A, the one with the glass showing, will enter into end B with the open lead. If you are working alone, take a piece of masking tape and wrap it around the piece to hold it in place. Then solder the final joint, top and bottom, inside and outside. Now you are ready to oxidize the soldering points. Use the same technique as in previous lesson for oxidizing, cementing and whiting. You are now ready to put in the electrical hardware according to instructions appearing later, and hang the lamp. Note: For variation A, use the same method of assembling. For B, C and D, the only variation is that you will need to cut the patterns with different templates and allow for the heart of the lead. Assemble each section as an individual panel (variations B and C). Repeat the procedure of steps 3 and 4 until all pieces are assembled, then put lead on top and bottom as previously explained. For variation C, repeat steps 2, 3 and 4 until you have finished the shade. Then as before, set the lead in top and bottom with the same technique as previously used and finish the lamp. For variation D, use the same technique of assembling as variation B.

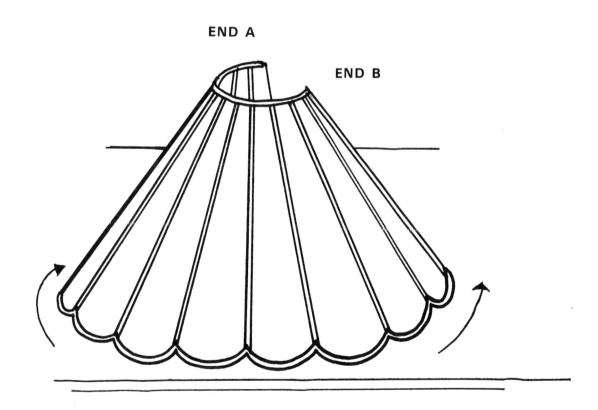

END A

END B

FIG. 38

VARIATION "B"

STEP #1   STEP #2   STEP #3   STEP #4

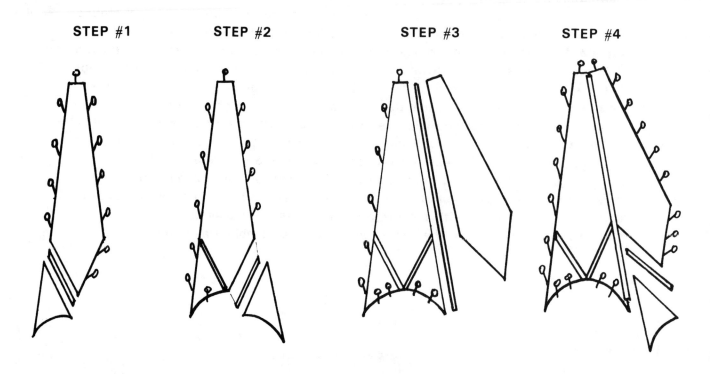

VARIATION "C"

STEP #1   STEP #2   STEP #3   STEP #4

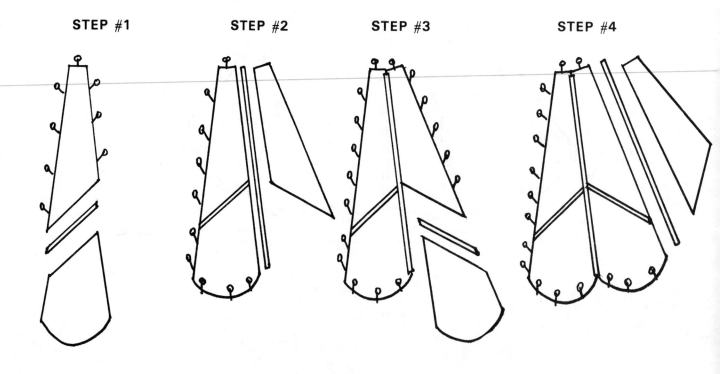

LESSON 6
TWELVE-SIDED LAMP WITH SKIRT AND CROWN

INSTRUCTIONS FOR ASSEMBLING:

Assemble the twelve pieces of the body, using the same technique as in Lesson 5 (figure 34, Figure 36, Figure 37). Solder and set aside.

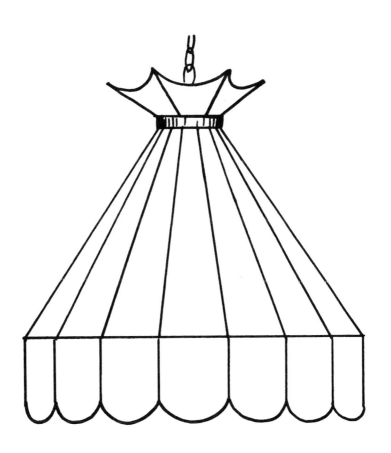

**12 SIDES LAMP
WITH "CROWN"
AND SKIRT**

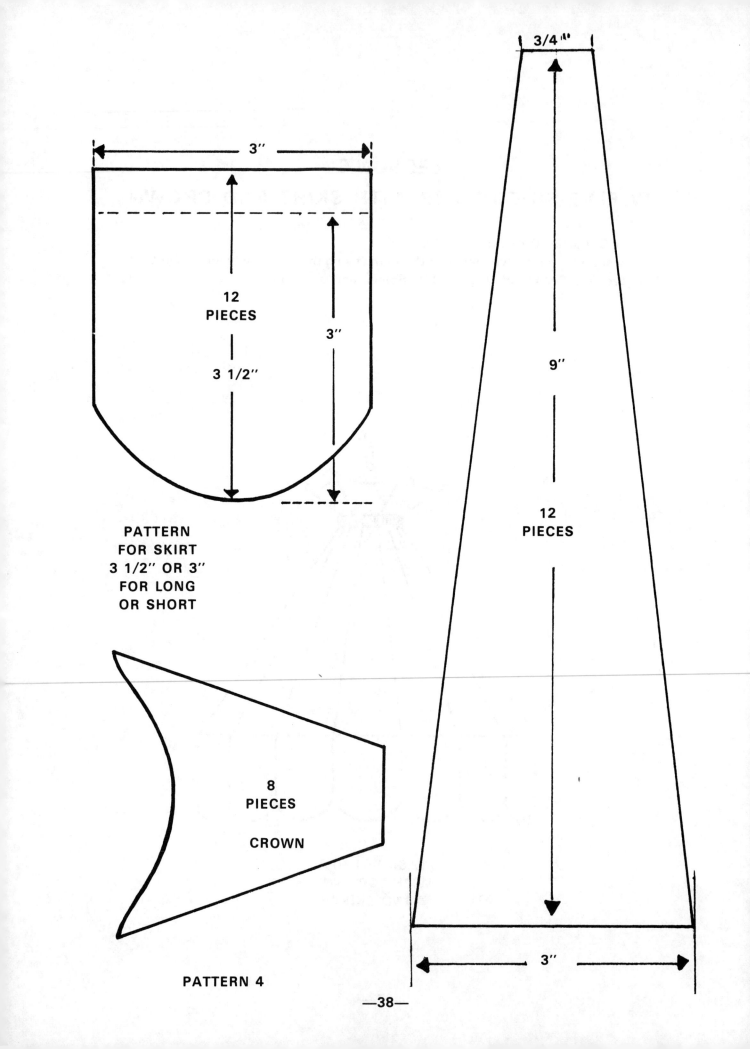

3"

12
PIECES

3 1/2"

3"

PATTERN
FOR SKIRT
3 1/2" OR 3"
FOR LONG
OR SHORT

8
PIECES

CROWN

PATTERN 4

3/4"

9"

12
PIECES

3"

ASSEMBLING THE SKIRT:

Place the twelve pieces of the skirt on the table and prepare for assembling. Nail a piece of wood 3/4" x 3/4" x 52" to the work table. Place a strip of lead against the wood and nail at one end. Start leading, using the same technique; however, instead of working in a semi-circle you will be working in a straight line (see Figure 39). After you have assembled all of the pieces of the skirt, push the lead into the bottom, following the curves as per Figure 40, allowing 1/8" at one end. After soldering, bend to form a circle and solder the ends together.

Now, turn the body upside down and work the skirt into it. If you have done everything correctly, the skirt should fit perfectly. Solder in the inside of this assembly at one point, work around the fitting and solder at another point. Continue doing this until you have all points soldered. Then clean, and another lamp is ready for the electrical parts to be added.

ASSEMBLING THE CROWN:

Cut eight pieces of the crown pattern as in pattern 3. Then follow the same procedure for assembling as used to assemble the body. You will be working with a semi-circle (see Figure 41).

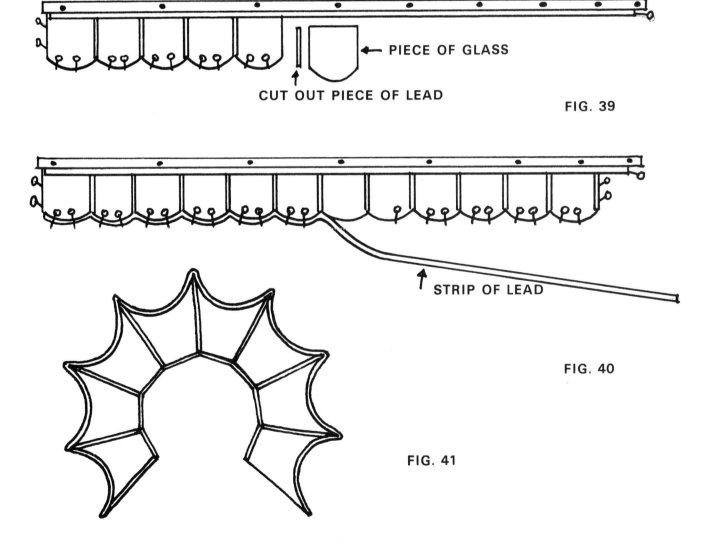

← PIECE OF GLASS

CUT OUT PIECE OF LEAD

FIG. 39

↑ STRIP OF LEAD

FIG. 40

FIG. 41

LESSON 7

SIXTEEN SIDED LAMP WITH CROWN, SKIRT, AND TWO SECTIONED BODY

In this lesson there will be instructions to make a sixteen sided lamp with crown, skirt and two sectional body which will creat an angle in the body. This pattern is very flexible and will allow you to design your own lamp with its own original shape, height and angularity.

To draw this pattern you will have to visulalize it first by using this simple rule; the taller the lower section of the body, the shorter the lamp would be; the taller the upper section of the body, the more elongated the lamp would be. To experiment with this pattern see figure 42 and follow the drawing instructions for drawing your own pattern.

Draw a vertical line X_1-X_2 and choose two points along that line, points A and C. The distance between these two points will be the approximate height of the pattern. Then draw horizontal lines Q_1-Q_2 and B_1-B_2 from Points A and C respectively. Along these lines choose Points A_1 and A_2, B_1 and B_2 which should be of equal distance from Points A and C respectively. Line A_1-A_2 and B_1-B_2 will be the width of the body section. Of course these points are measured to whatever shape and size of lamp you desire to make. Then choose a point between points A and C and call it Point B. This point will constitute the shape of the upper body section in regard to height and width of the lamp. The closer Point B to Point C, the taller the body will be; and the further Point B from Point C, the shorter the body of the lamp will be.

This is the time to make your decision about the shape of the lamp. After you have choosen Point B, then draw a horizontal line through that point which will be line W_1-W_2 then connect Points B_1 and B_2 with vertical lines to line Q_1-Q_2, also draw diagonal line from Points B_1 and B_2 to Points A_1 and A_2. These lines are called Y_1-Y_2 and Z_1-Z_2 respectively. At this time measure the distant between the points of intersection of Lines B_1-Q_1 and Y_1-Y_2 along the line W_1-W_2. Do the same thing on the right side of drawing. Find the mid-point on the measured sections of these lines and call it Points D and F respectively. Correct these new points to Points A_1, B_1 and A_2, B_2 respectively. This will be the pattern for the body section of the lamp. Your cutting lines will be A_1-A_2, B_1-B_2, D-F, A_1-D, B_1-D, A_2-F and B_2-F. See figure 42.

ASSEMBLY:

The assembly of this lamp is the same as the assembly instructions in Lessons 5 and 6. You can create as many variations in skirt and body as you may desire. Pattern 5 is a very good pattern to assemble. It also has several simple variations of its skirt, see Pattern 6. The peacock variation is a very interesting pattern to make for those who like to attempt making a more difficult but colorful lamp, see Pattern 7.

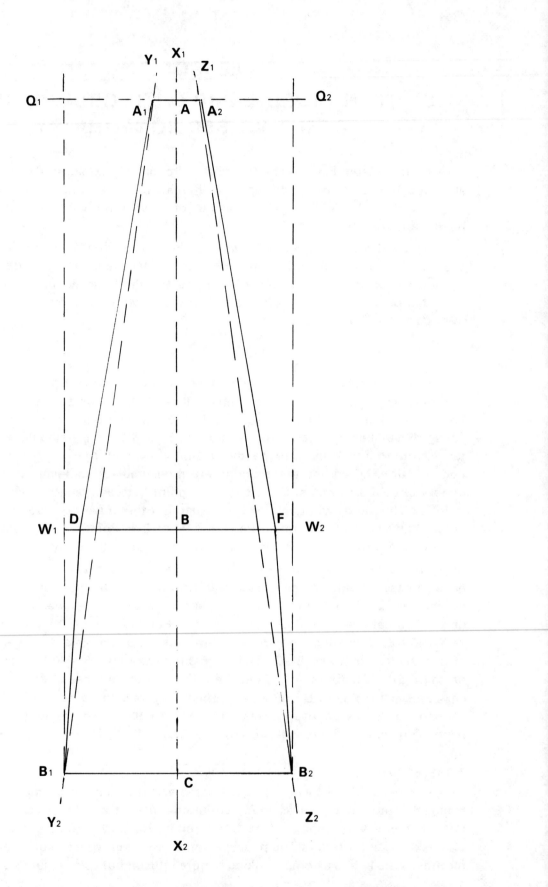

FIG. 42

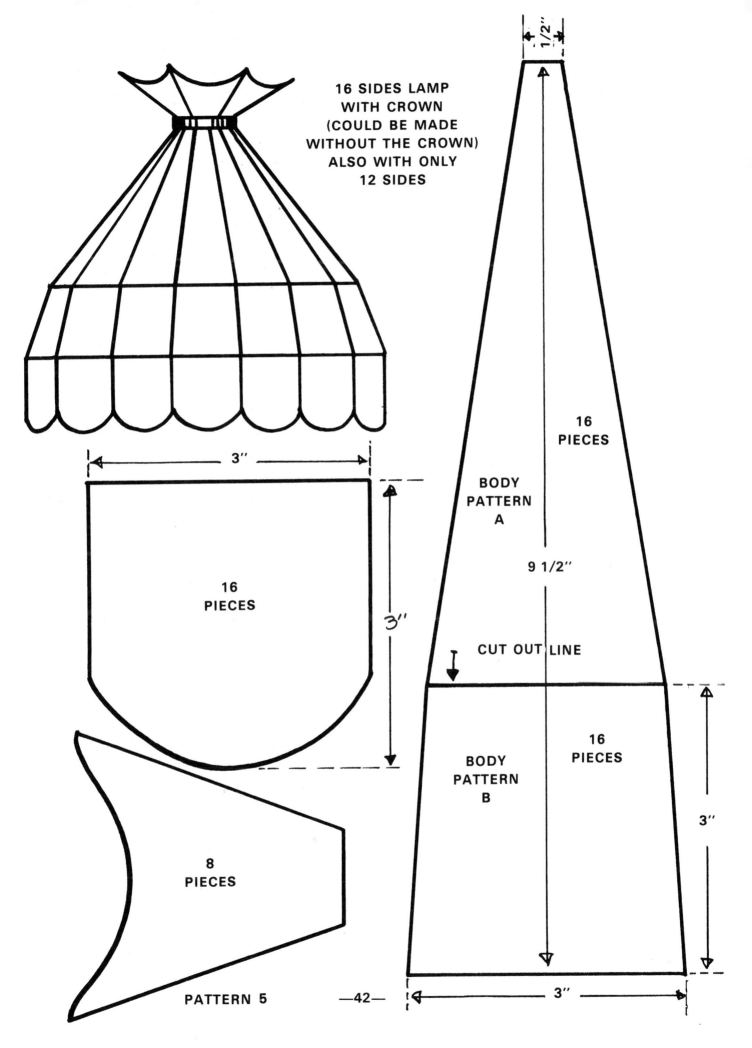

16 SIDES LAMP
WITH CROWN
(COULD BE MADE
WITHOUT THE CROWN)
ALSO WITH ONLY
12 SIDES

1/2"

16
PIECES

BODY
PATTERN
A

9 1/2"

CUT OUT LINE

3"

16
PIECES

3"

16
PIECES

BODY
PATTERN
B

16
PIECES

3"

8
PIECES

PATTERN 5

—42—

3"

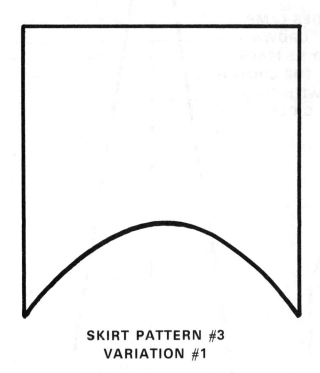

SKIRT PATTERN #3
VARIATION #1

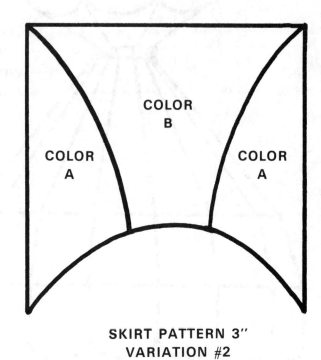

SKIRT PATTERN 3"
VARIATION #2

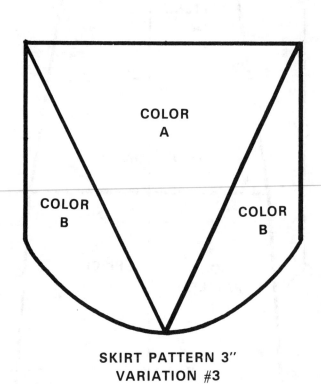

SKIRT PATTERN 3"
VARIATION #3

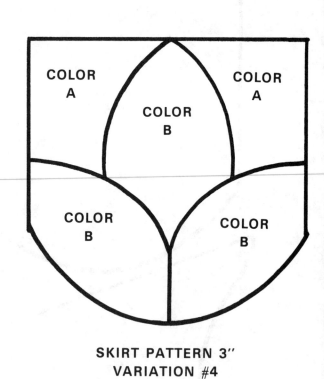

SKIRT PATTERN 3"
VARIATION #4

PATTERN 6

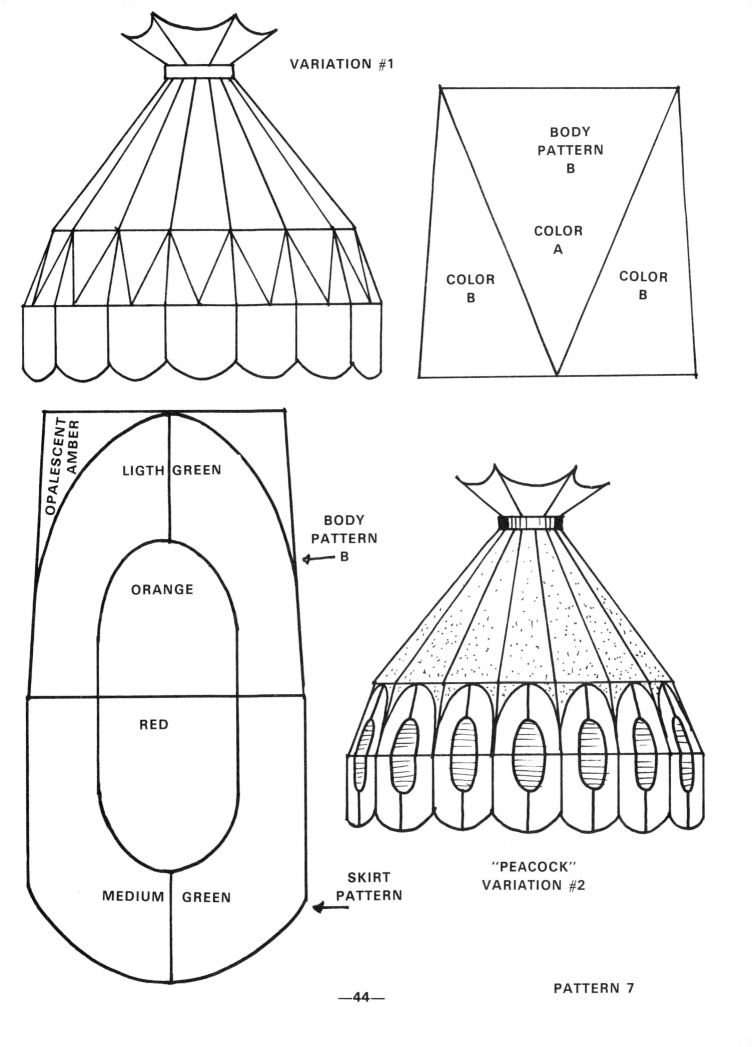

VARIATION #1

BODY
PATTERN
B

COLOR
A

COLOR
B

COLOR
B

OPALESCENT AMBER

LIGTH GREEN

ORANGE

RED

MEDIUM GREEN

BODY
PATTERN
← B

SKIRT
PATTERN

"PEACOCK"
VARIATION #2

—44—

PATTERN 7

LESSON 8
TERRARIUMS

Because of the nature of terrariums, they must be sealed completely with solder and caulking to effectively make them waterproof.

LANTERN TERRARIUMS:

Cut the patterns as illustrated in Pattern 9, then cut the required number of pieces of glass for each section. Assemble sections A, B, C and D, following the sequence shown in figure 43, and use the same techniques previously described in making the twelve-sided lamp. Sections A and D will be assembled by using the semi-circle assembly technique previously described for the crown of the twelve-sided lamp (Figure 41).

LANTERN TERRARIUM

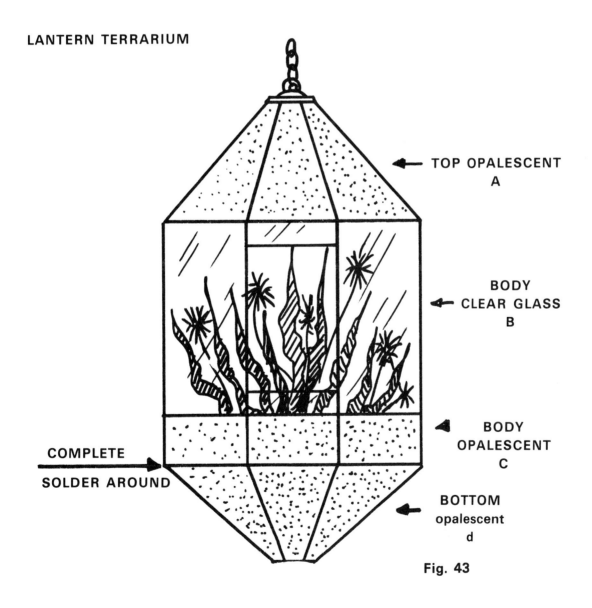

TOP OPALESCENT
A

BODY
CLEAR GLASS
B

BODY
OPALESCENT
C

COMPLETE
SOLDER AROUND

BOTTOM
opalescent
d

Fig. 43

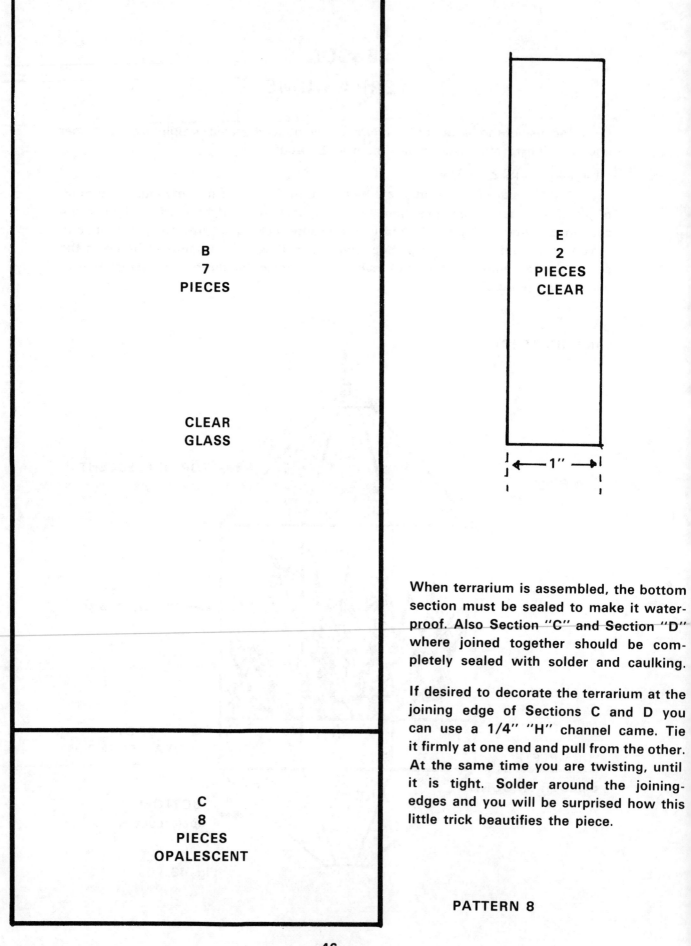

B
7
PIECES

CLEAR
GLASS

E
2
PIECES
CLEAR

|← 1″ →|

C
8
PIECES
OPALESCENT

When terrarium is assembled, the bottom section must be sealed to make it water-proof. Also Section "C" and Section "D" where joined together should be completely sealed with solder and caulking.

If desired to decorate the terrarium at the joining edge of Sections C and D you can use a 1/4″ "H" channel came. Tie it firmly at one end and pull from the other. At the same time you are twisting, until it is tight. Solder around the joining-edges and you will be surprised how this little trick beautifies the piece.

PATTERN 8

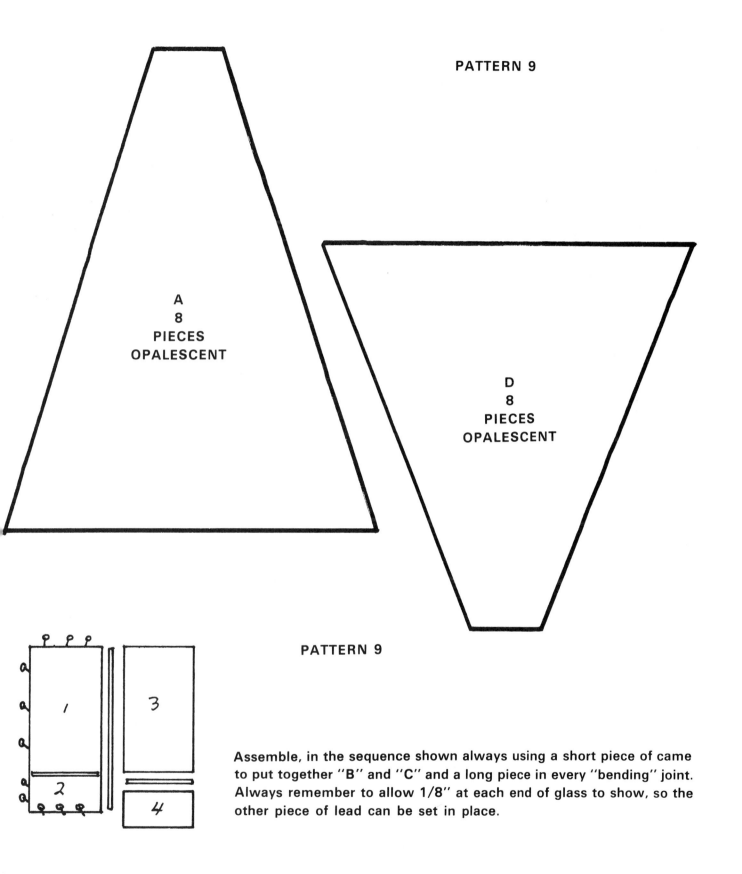

A
8
PIECES
OPALESCENT

D
8
PIECES
OPALESCENT

PATTERN 9

Assemble, in the sequence shown always using a short piece of came to put together "B" and "C" and a long piece in every "bending" joint. Always remember to allow 1/8" at each end of glass to show, so the other piece of lead can be set in place.

Assemble, Section "A" and "D" in the semi-circle technique previously explained.

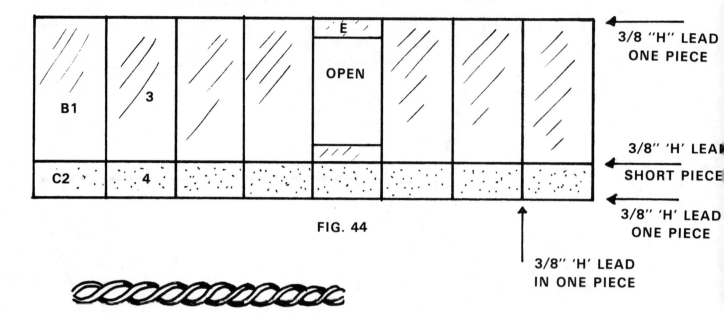

				E			
B1	3			OPEN			
C2	4						

3/8 "H" LEAD
ONE PIECE

3/8" 'H' LEAI
SHORT PIECE

3/8" 'H' LEAD
ONE PIECE

3/8" 'H' LEAD
IN ONE PIECE

FIG. 44

Actual size 1/4". "H" came twisted to
use for dressing.

For the "closing bottom piece of Section "D" after you have it assembled, turn it over,
trace the inside to make a pattern, add 1/16" around. Cut out your piece, use a "U"
channel to lead-around, then open the inside of the "H" channel in the bottom and set
the piece in, be sure to solder all the way around.

Before assembling Sections A, B, C and D together to complete the terrarium,
be sure all the lead channels are straight and sufficiently open to accommodate the
sections for fitting and soldering. This type terrarium can be hung as is or electrified.

TABLE TERRARIUMS (OPEN TERRARIUMS)

This type terrarium has a flat bottom and is ideal for using on tables. Cut the
templates according to the patterns in Pattern 10. Then cut the required number of
pieces of glass and assemble according to illustration figure 44. Use a 3/16" U
channel at the top and 3/8" round H channel everywhere else. Assemble the eight
pieces of pattern A and the eight pieces of pattern B. Then join section A to section
B and solder. Use the completed octagonal shape as a pattern. Set it on a piece
of paper and draw a line along the inside dimension and then add 1/8" to the line.
Use this pattern to cut the bottom piece of glass. Set a 3/16" U channel lead came
around the bottom piece. Then turn the octagon assembly over and be sure the H
channel is open all around; set in the bottom piece and solder all around as shown
in figure 46. In addition to the pattern variations given in Patterns 11 and 12, you
may change the basic pattern dimensions and achieve further variations.

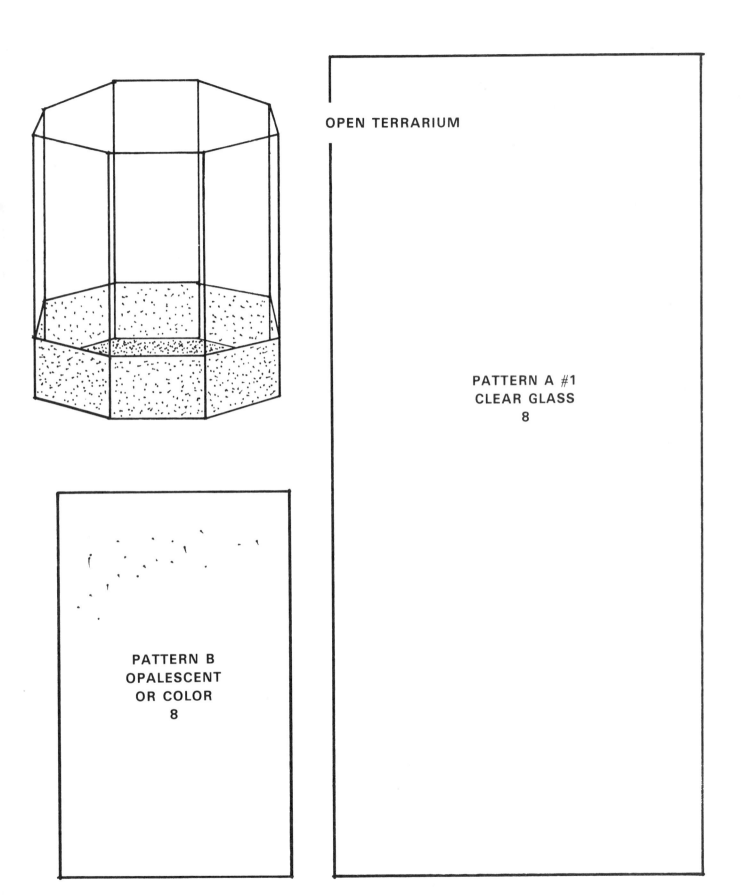

OPEN TERRARIUM

PATTERN A #1
CLEAR GLASS
8

PATTERN B
OPALESCENT
OR COLOR
8

PATTERN 10

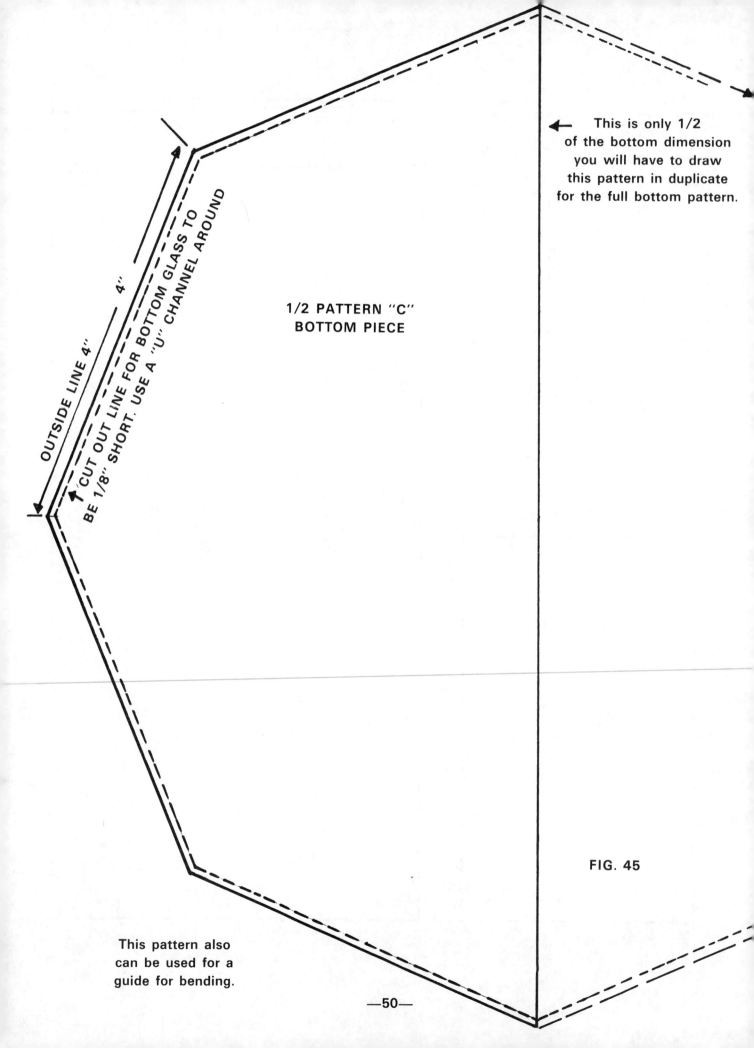

This is only 1/2 of the bottom dimension you will have to draw this pattern in duplicate for the full bottom pattern.

OUTSIDE LINE 4"

4"

CUT OUT LINE FOR BOTTOM GLASS TO BE 1/8" SHORT. USE A "U" CHANNEL AROUND

1/2 PATTERN "C"
BOTTOM PIECE

FIG. 45

This pattern also can be used for a guide for bending.

SECTION PATTERN "A" #3

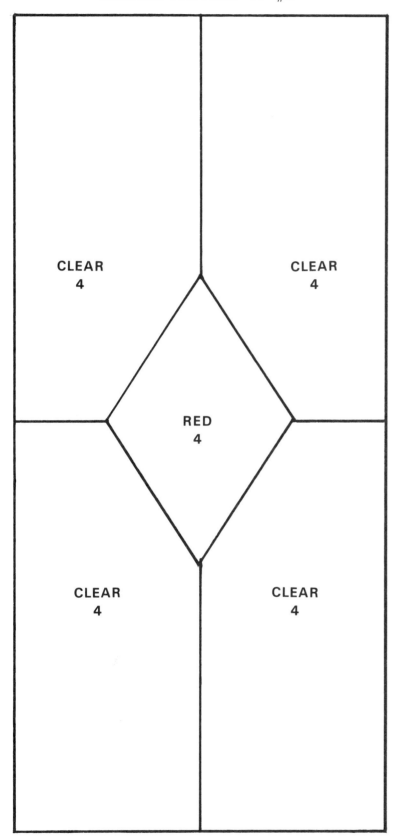

"DIAMOND PATTERN"

You can use Pattern "A" #1 with Pattern "A" #2 or Pattern "A" #1 with Pattern "A" #3 or Pattern "A" 2 with Pattern "A" 3.

COMBINATIONS
PATTERN #1 ONLY
PATTERN #2 ONLY
PATTERN #3 ONLY
PATTERN #1 WITH PATTERN #2
PATTERN #1 WITH PATTERN #3
PATTERN #2 WITH PATTERN #3

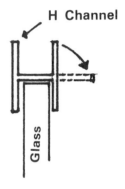

FIG. 46

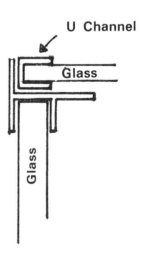

PATTERN 11

—51—

SECTION PATTERN "A" #2

'OPEN TERRARIUM'
Variation "A"
Of the eight sides use the Tulip Pattern in four and the Diamond Pattern in the other four sections. Be sure when making the templates to cut out the allowance for the heart of the lead.

You can also build this terrarium in copper-foil, but use a 3/8" came at the outside

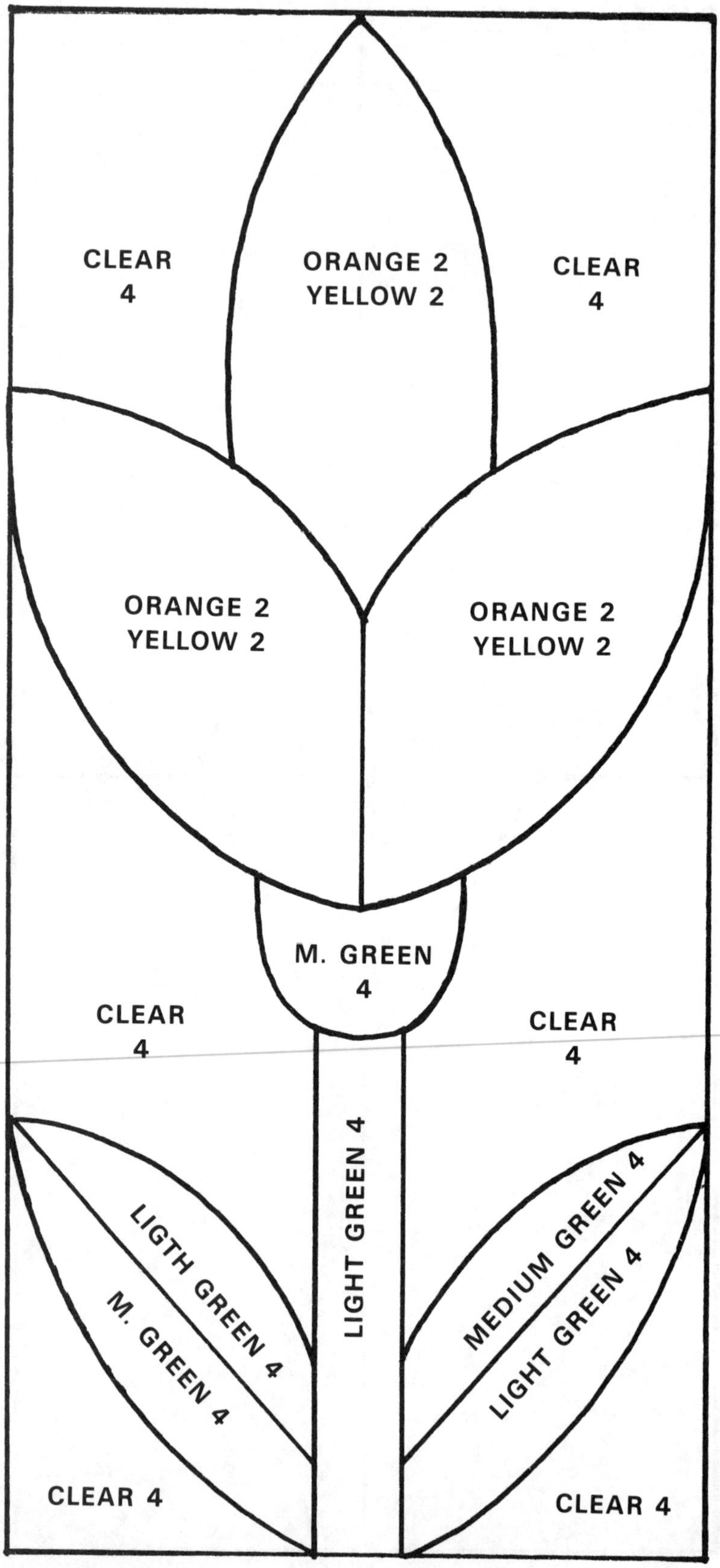

"TULIP PATTERN"

PATTERN 12

CLEAR
4

ORANGE 2
YELLOW 2

CLEAR
4

ORANGE 2
YELLOW 2

ORANGE 2
YELLOW 2

M. GREEN
4

CLEAR
4

CLEAR
4

LIGTH GREEN 4

M. GREEN 4

LIGHT GREEN 4

MEDIUM GREEN 4

LIGHT GREEN 4

CLEAR 4

CLEAR 4

LESSON 9
12" TIFFANY STYLE LAMP USING COPPER FOIL TECHNIQUE
(With 3 Skirt Variations)

The technique of copper foiling is simple and is used mainly in building Tiffany style lamps. Best results for this type of lamp are achieved by the use of a mold. You can make your own mold using paper mache and a family-size bowl, or you can buy one from suppliers. I use Nervo Studios in Berkeley, California. For this technique you will also need cooper foil. This material comes in rolls of different sizes, the most common being 1/4", but it also comes in widths of 3/8" and 1/2". Copper foil is manufactured by Borden's Chemical Company, 1700 Winnetka Road, Northfield, Illinois 60093, telephone number (312) 446-0622. You can write them for the address of the nearest distributor in your locality. Copper foil tape comes with an adhesive back that sticks to the glass. After you have made or bought your 12" mold, copy the patterns on a bristol board, cut out the templates and cut your glass. The only thing you must remember at this point is that the better the quality of the opalescent glass that you select, the better the quality of the lamp. Select one color for the body and after you have cut all the pieces for it, wrap them in foil, being sure the glass is balanced in the center of the foil as in figure 47.

TECHNIQUE FOR FOILING

1. Cut a length of copper foil that will cover the perimeter of the glass.

2. Starting in one corner, pull the adhesive paper out enough to let you foil one side of the piece, being sure your fingers do not touch the back of the copper foil because the adhesive is very sensitive. Pull the tape, center your piece of glass, bend the corner against the glass. Having completed the copper foiling of one side of your piece of glass, repeat the same procedure until you have all sides foiled.

3. Cut off any excess and press both protruding portions of foil against the two faces of the glass, trying to get the copper foil as flat as possible all around (edges and faces).

4. Repeat this process until you have all the pieces of the body foiled.

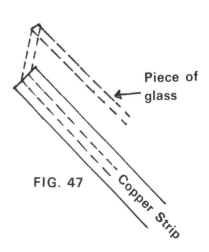

Piece of glass

FIG. 47   Copper Strip

LESSON 9   PATTERN 13

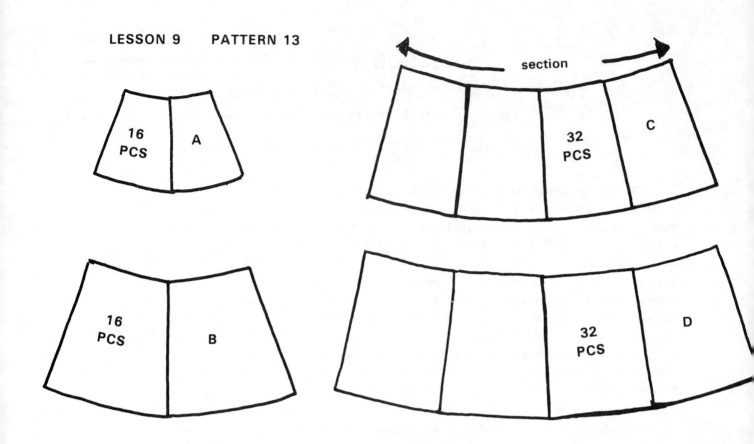

Section A, B - repeat 8 times (16 pcs)
C, D, E, F and G - repeat 8 times (32 pcs.)

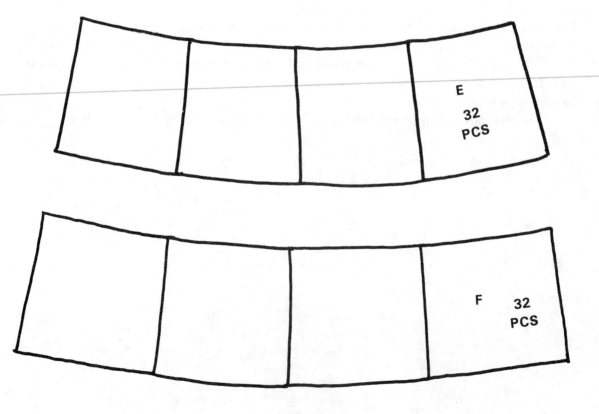

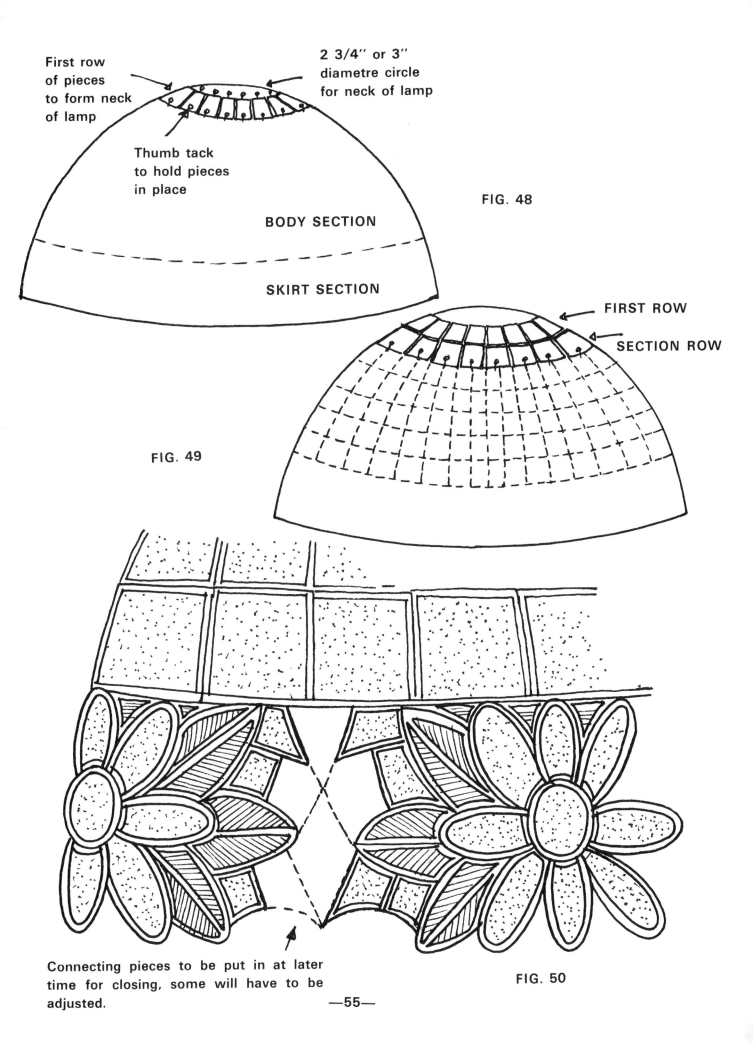

First row of pieces to form neck of lamp

2 3/4" or 3" diametre circle for neck of lamp

Thumb tack to hold pieces in place

FIG. 48

BODY SECTION

SKIRT SECTION

FIRST ROW

SECTION ROW

FIG. 49

Connecting pieces to be put in at later time for closing, some will have to be adjusted.

FIG. 50

TECHNIQUE FOR ASSEMBLING

1. From the center of the mold draw a circle of 2 3/4" diameter; this will be your neck opening for the lamp. You can use a compass with legs open at 1 3/8" for your radius.

2. Starting right below the neck circle, start assembling the copper foiled pieces of the first row and tack solder as you go. Use thumb tacks to secure them in place and tack solder as much as you need.

3. You probably will have to adjust some pieces to conform to the shape of your mold in order to get the sixteen pieces of the first row in Figure 48. Usually this can be done by making your adjustment to the last piece in the row.

4. Now start the second row, using the same technique of tack soldering and adjusting.

5. After you have the first and second rows in, make a mark where they fit on the mold. Take them off the mold and bead solder the inside and solder the outside too. Doing this will cause the shape you have formed to be permanent.

6. Now that you have the first two rows assembled, proceed with the other rows, using the same technique until you reach the skirt, Figure 49.

7. When you have finished the body of the lamp you are ready to start assembling the skirt section. To do this, cut the templates, the glass pieces, and foil. Assemble each of the four sections separately on the table, using the bead solder technique on the outside only. Leave out several of the last connecting pieces of the skirt assembly for final adjustment, Figure 50.

8. After you have assembled the skirt sections, solder them to the body, taking care to conform the sections to the shape of the mold. After you have secured them in place, solder the inside to get a permanent shape, Figure 50.

9. Now you are ready to finish the closing of the lamp. Adjust by cutting the connecting pieces left out to conform to the opening you have left, and finish soldering.

10. After you have finished the assembling of the lamp on the mold, you should go over the soldering joints, trying to smooth them as much as you can. This can best be done by using an 80 or 100 watt soldering iron.

11. Add the electrical parts according to the illustration of electrical components, Figure 50 and it is ready for lighting.

Patterns 13 and 14 are the necessary sections of the body and skirt of the Tiffany style lamp. Sections A, B, C, D, E, and F should be assembled in a desending order from top of the mold to the point where body meets the flowered pattern skirt, as in Pattern 14. Pattern 15 will give skirt variation for Tiffany style lamp.

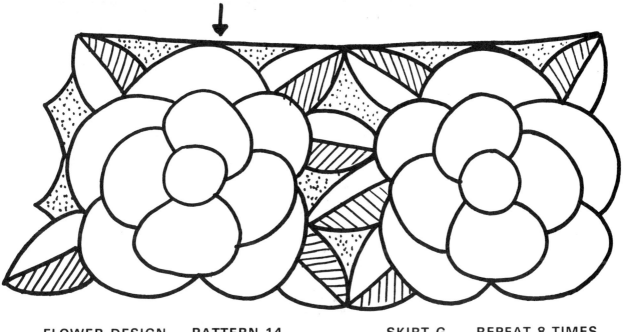

FLOWER DESIGN   PATTERN 14   SKIRT G   REPEAT 8 TIMES

GRAPES PATTERN

PATTERN 15 VARIATION A
SKIRT - REPEAT 8 TIMES (G)

TULIP PATTERN   —57—

PATTERN 15
VARIATION B
SKIRT- REPEAT 8 TIMES (G)

LESSON 10
ELECTRICAL COMPONENTS AND
MISCELLANEOUS IDEAS

This lesson is to tie together any loose ends and to open the door for miscellaneous ideas and designs which will be fun using techniques acquired in the previous lessons.

Electrical: I have referred to electrical components many times in the previous chapters dealings with lamps. The illustrations shown in figure 51 and figure 52 clearly show the necessary parts needed to electrify your lamps. The parts are drawn in the proper order for assembly and should be referred to for all your electrical assembling.

"ELECTRICAL COMPONENTS"

These are suggested electrical part without a "crown"

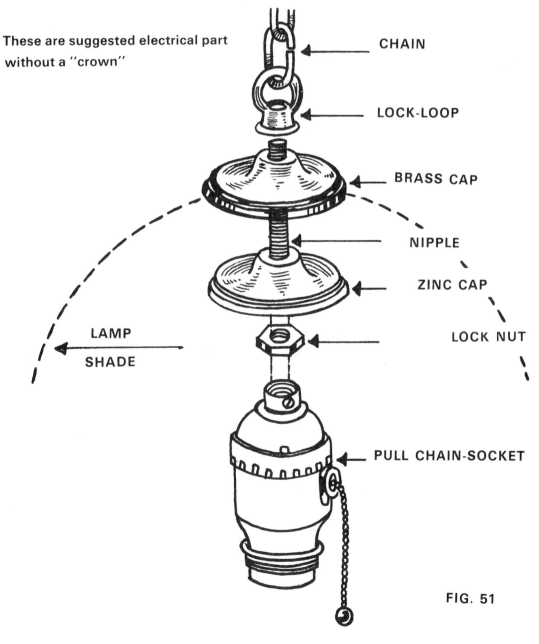

CHAIN

LOCK-LOOP

BRASS CAP

NIPPLE

ZINC CAP

LAMP
SHADE

LOCK NUT

PULL CHAIN-SOCKET

FIG. 51

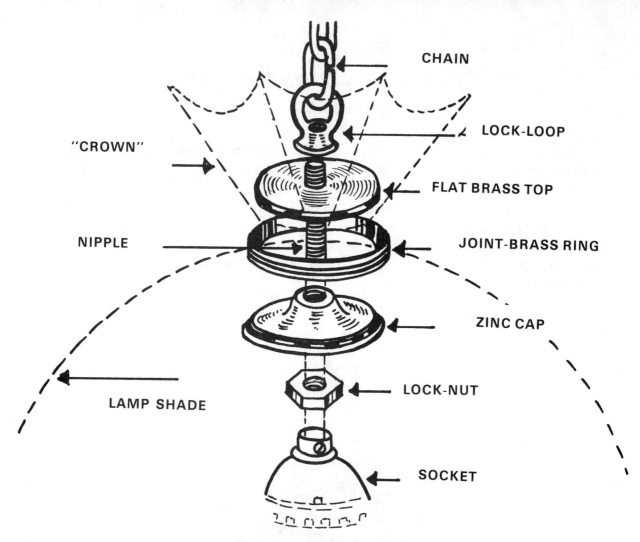

CHAIN

LOCK-LOOP

"CROWN"

FLAT BRASS TOP

NIPPLE

JOINT-BRASS RING

ZINC CAP

LAMP SHADE

LOCK-NUT

SOCKET

THESE ARE SUGGESTED ELECTRICAL PARTS
FOR ASSEMBLING A LAMP WITH "CROWN"

FIG. 52

MISCELLANEOUS IDEAS:

Using the basic ideas previously explained in the construction of the various lamps worked on in the previous lessons, you can now make the beautiful "Floral Pattern" six sided lamp as shown in pattern 16. You will note that this lamp may be made by using either the lead came or copper foil method.

The skirt pattern is illustrated in pattern 16A and the body pattern is shown in pattern 16B. Number the various pieces for the skirt and the body as previously explained. The top section is shown in FIG. 52 A and should also be numbered. Then cut out the numbered pieces and you will be ready to begin cutting the glass. Be sure to remember that your method of cutting out the patterns will be determined by whether you choose lead came or copper foil for your construction technique. Detailed instructions are given in conjunction with the patterns for both methods, see Figure 54.

There are also variations of both the body and skirt patterns as shown in Patterns 16C and 16D. You will certainly enjoy the finished product as this is one of the most attractive lamps that can be made.

"FLORAL PATTERN 6 SIDED LAMP

"COOPER FOILING: Set 2 strips of wood 3/4" x 3/4" x 10" or 1" x 1" x 10" at the edge of the assembling Pattern #1 following the angle (see Fig 53).

Copper foil all the pieces, place them in their position in the pattern, nail the border, to hold them in their place, and solder, be sure you build a good bead of solder in every line, you have to remember that you are building a shape came lead, turn around, and repeat the soldering.

Repeat the same proceedure with the pattern of the Skirt #2 (Figure 52), and after you have finished, attach Section "A" (Body) and Section "B" (Skirt) together solder and set aside. Repeat, until you have all of the Sections "A" and "B" attached. Then assemble the attached sections two at a time with solder, until all of the attached body and skirt sections are assembled.

Assemble the "top section" and solder to the body, always remembering to buld a good bead of solder, inside and outside.

"FLORAL PATTERN" 6 SIDED LAMP

CAME LEAD ASSEMBLING: To assemble this lamp with came lead, use a 1/8" or 3/16" H Channel. When cutting the pattern, remember to cut out an allowance for the heart of the lead-came, so the assembled pieces will fit.

Use the same technique as explained in the first part of this book. For the bottom part of the skirt, use a "U" Channel, if possible build each section individually, and then assemble all the "skirt" sections. Do the same with the body sections, and when finished, fit the "body" to the "skirt".

**"FLORAL PATTERN" 6 SIDES
COPPER FOIL OR LEAD**

PATTERN 16

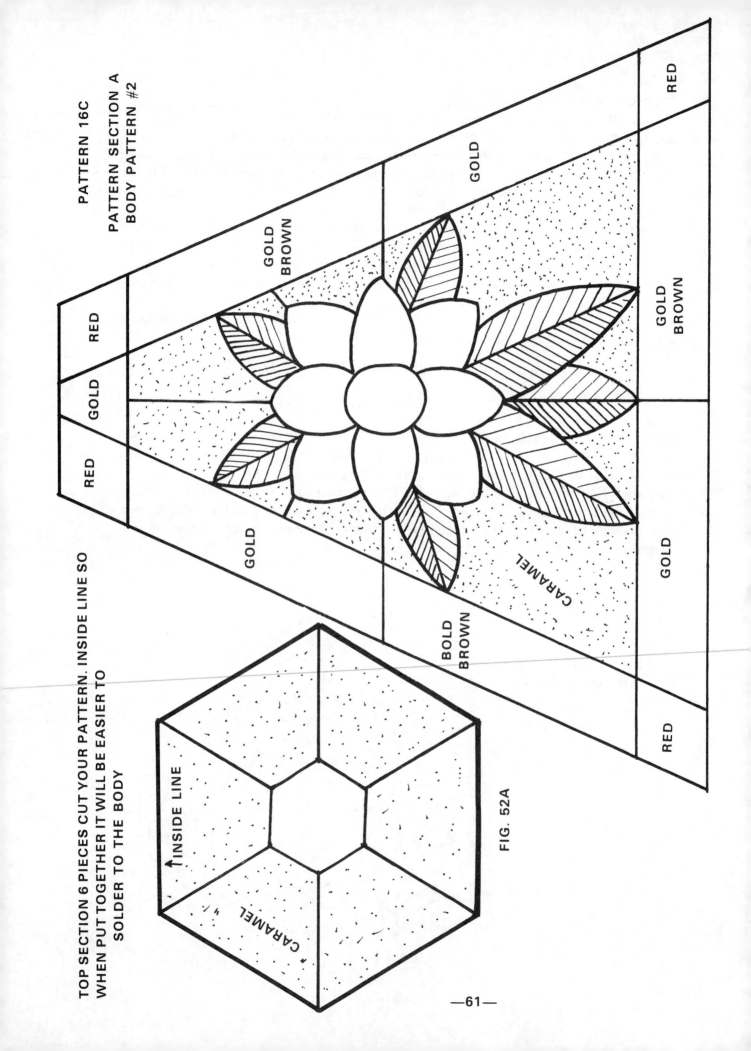

PATTERN 16C

PATTERN SECTION A
BODY PATTERN #2

TOP SECTION 6 PIECES CUT YOUR PATTERN. INSIDE LINE SO
WHEN PUT TOGETHER IT WILL BE EASIER TO
SOLDER TO THE BODY

RED

GOLD

RED

GOLD

GOLD
BROWN

GOLD

GOLD
BROWN

RED

GOLD

CARAMEL

BOLD
BROWN

RED

INSIDE LINE

CARAMEL

FIG. 52A

—61—

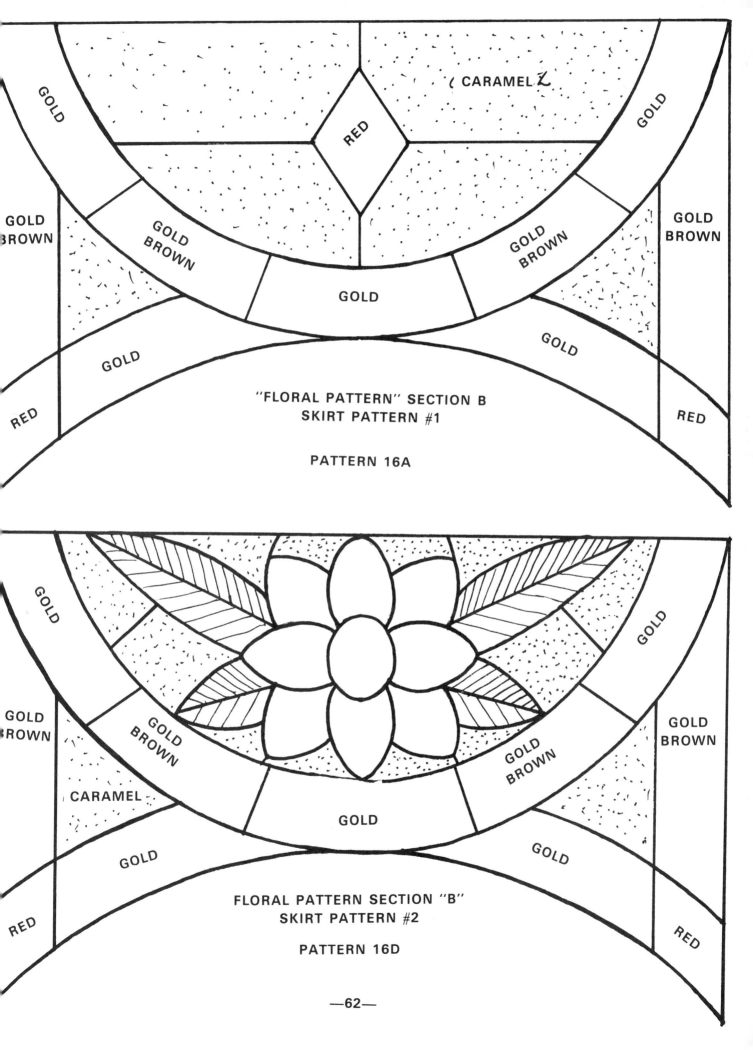

"FLORAL PATTERN" SECTION B
SKIRT PATTERN #1

PATTERN 16A

FLORAL PATTERN SECTION "B"
SKIRT PATTERN #2

PATTERN 16D

—62—

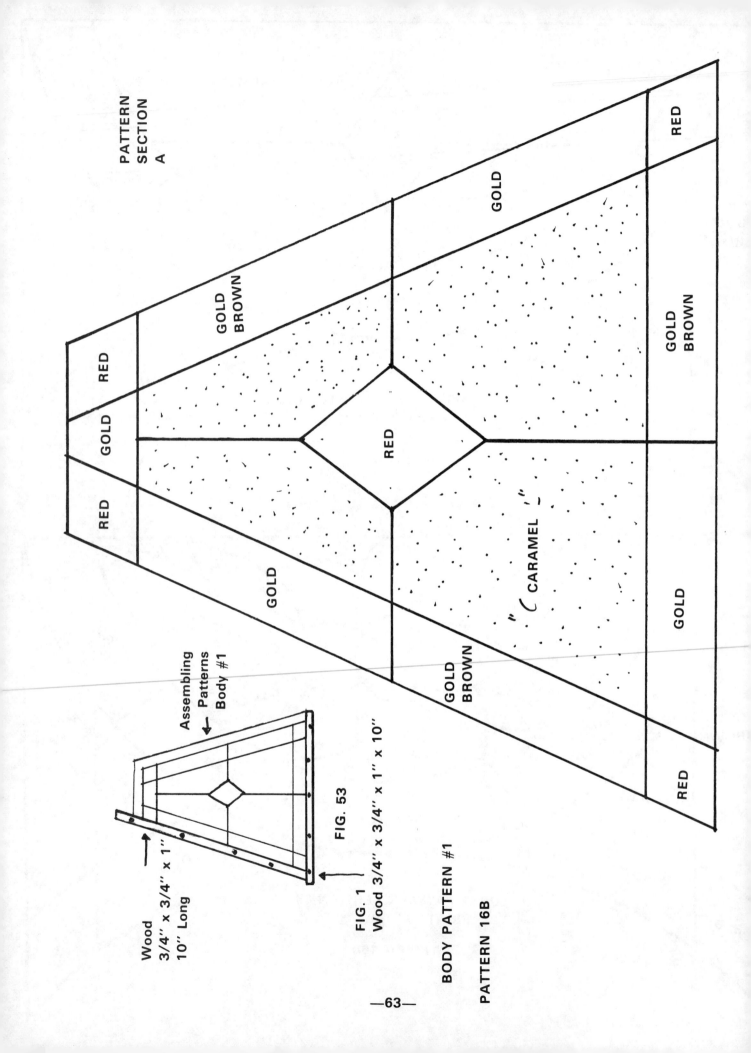

PATTERN SECTION A

RED

GOLD BROWN

GOLD

RED

GOLD BROWN

GOLD

RED

GOLD

GOLD BROWN

RED

RED

GOLD

CARAMEL

Assembling
Patterns
Body #1

Wood
3/4" x 3/4" x 1"
10" Long

FIG. 1
Wood 3/4" x 3/4" x 1" x 10"

FIG. 53

BODY PATTERN #1

PATTERN 16B

—63—

FIG. 54

Strip of wood

Assembling Pattern Skirt #2

FRONT LAWN LIGHT: LEAD OR COPPER FOIL

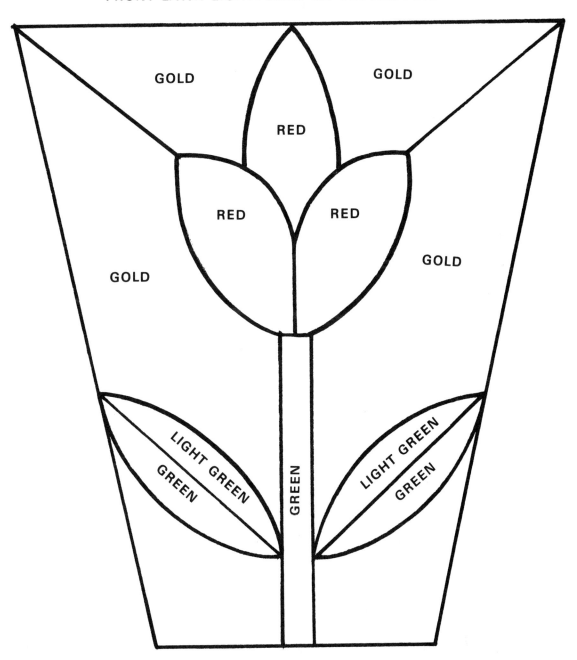

GOLD

GOLD

RED

RED

RED

GOLD

GOLD

LIGHT GREEN

GREEN

GREEN

LIGHT GREEN

GREEN

PATTERN 17

Patterns 17 and 17 A are pattern suggestions for glass panels in outside lawn lights. These patterns are standard size for most outside lights. However, I would suggest that you take out a glass panel and check the dimensions with the illustrations to be sure it is the same. If there is a difference in size, you are now qualified to draw your own pattern to fit your light. Any number of different designs will come readily to you as you work on such a project. You should keep one thing in mind with outside lights; the panel that faces a walkway or any other area to be lighted should be clear glass.

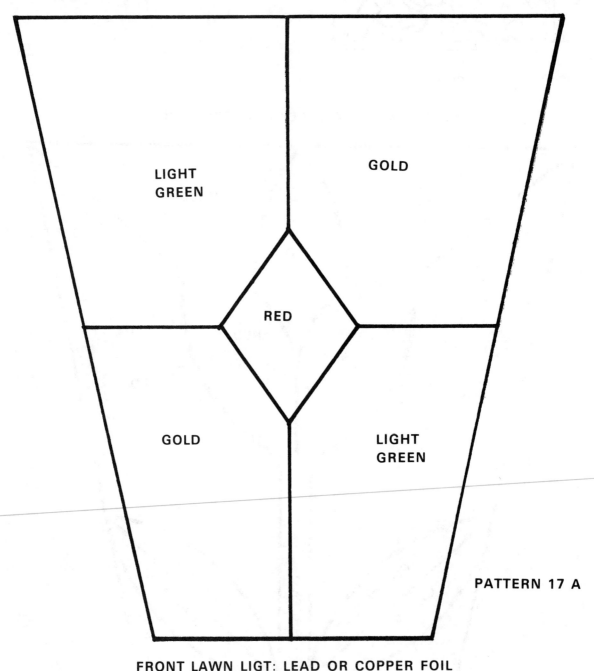

PATTERN 17 A

FRONT LAWN LIGT: LEAD OR COPPER FOIL

Panel or pictures in various colors and types of glass can be made to hang in windows. A fish is illustrated in Pattern 18. Birds, rabbits and almost any animal may be used. Keep the basic design simple and arrange your pieces without too many complex cuts and you will be pleasantly surprised with how quickly you can complete such projects.

HERE ARE A FEW IDEAS!

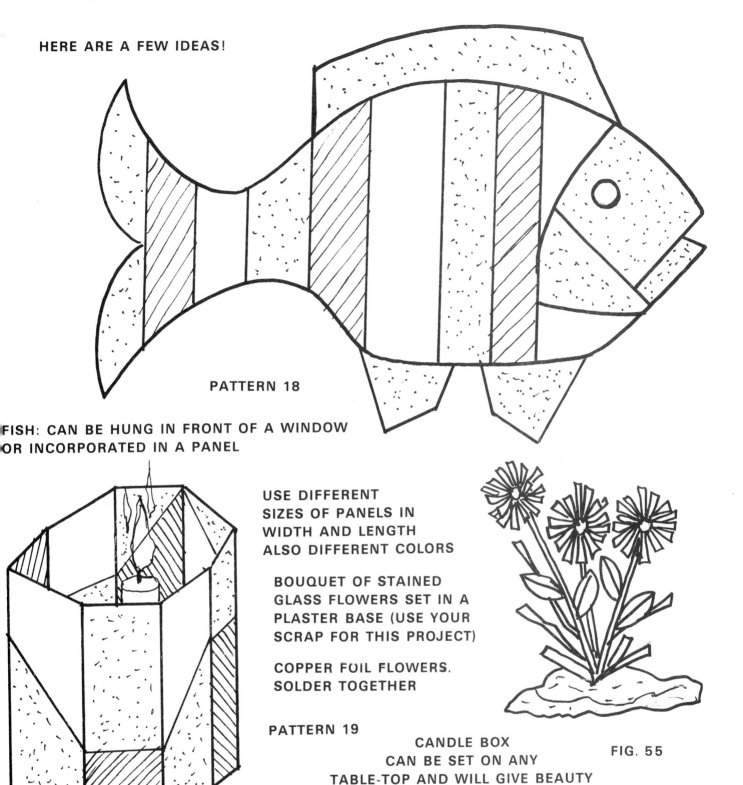

PATTERN 18

FISH: CAN BE HUNG IN FRONT OF A WINDOW
OR INCORPORATED IN A PANEL

USE DIFFERENT
SIZES OF PANELS IN
WIDTH AND LENGTH
ALSO DIFFERENT COLORS

BOUQUET OF STAINED
GLASS FLOWERS SET IN A
PLASTER BASE (USE YOUR
SCRAP FOR THIS PROJECT)

COPPER FOIL FLOWERS.
SOLDER TOGETHER

PATTERN 19

CANDLE BOX
CAN BE SET ON ANY
TABLE-TOP AND WILL GIVE BEAUTY
WHEN CANDLE IS LIGHTED

FIG. 55

Another idea whereby you can create beautiful accessories for your home is illustrated in Pattern 19. Candle boxes such as shown in the illustration can be made with any number of sides. Select the type you want and then cut cardboard templates and scotch tape together to be sure your design will assemble properly. Then design the sides and cut your glass. You can use either the copper foil or lead came method for assembling.

A bouquet of stained glass flowers can also be made as illustrated in Figure 55. The stems may vary in length anywhere from 6" to 10". Leaf and flower designs can vary depending on your own ideas. The flower can be three (3) dimensional with petals clustered at the center and coming out at different angles. The copper foil technique must be used to assemble such a bouquet. After the assembly of the flowers by soldering, the bouquet can be mounted on a plaster of paris base.

The ideas mentioned in this chapter can be varied and should stimulate your imagination to even more creative thoughts. All of the projects suggested in this chapter are good to make use of "scrap" pieces of glass left over from other projects.

Nearing the conclusion of this book, I give special thanks and credit to two of my students. They both attended my classes and learned the same techniques covered in these instructions. They are Don Crawford, who built the 12" Tiffany type lamp used on the cover illustration, and Kent Cooper, who built the 20" grape and flower lamp also illustrated. Their work has been used as illustrations as proof and encouragement, that, although all of you readers may be inexperienced in stained glass work just as Don and Kent were, faithful and diligent practice of the instructions given in these pages will produce beautiful work of equal quality.

Sometime in the near future there will be another instructional book ready for those successful in mastering the techniques taught in this beginner's course. It will be called "A Complete Course in Advanced Stained Glass Techniques."

I wish the readers of this book all of the success and pleasure that I feel sure they will have from successfully completing top-quality stained glass work.

PEPE MENDEZ